CALLED TO BE A NUISANCE

Betty Maher

Called To Be A Nuisance
Reflections from the fringe

the columba press

First published in 1997 by
the columba press
55a Spruce Avenue, Stillorgan Industrial Park
Blackrock, Co Dublin

Cover by Bill Bolger
Origination by The Columba Press
Printed in Ireland by Colour Books Ltd, Dublin

ISBN 1 85607 191 X

Acknowledgements

My thanks are due to Dr Brendan Lovett, SSC, for his incisive teaching, to Dr Gabriel Daly, OSA, for the courteous and generous giving of his time to thought-provoking and instructive discussion, and to two or three other stalwarts, anonymous by their own choice, for some meticulous proof-reading, correcting and suggesting. Any remaining errors are solely mine. The poem by E. E. Cummings is used by kind permission of W. W. Norton & Company, London.

Betty Maher
February 18, 1997
Feast of St Bernadette Soubrious

Contents

Contents

To the memory of my parents,
and to all who in the interest of truth ask questions

'Nothing can go on if we leave the table.'
Teilhard de Chardin, *The Phenomenon of Man*

Introduction

In ecclesiastical matters (and not only in those) for all of nearly 2,000 years women have, as I see it, almost always been considered nuisances if they as much as express an interest in having some input into the manner in which such matters are conducted. You only have to read a biography of someone like Teresa of Avila, or Catherine of Siena, or even the gentle Thérèse of Liseux, to see that their interest in and approach to church affairs caused enormous problems to the Powers That Were and that therefore those excellent women, and no doubt countless others besides, were put in a position of having to live with the knowledge that the very people with whom they wished to engage actually perceived them as profound nuisances. And that is not a great position to be in throughout one's life. It means that energy which might well be put to good use in the furtherance of the Word is oftentimes spent simply in justifying one's existence. A waste.

I believe that it is extremely hard for many men who live their lives in their chosen field of ministry to understand fully the pain some women feel today when they are perceived as nuisances just because they, like their male counterparts, wish to follow their calling – for example, to the ordained priesthood, or other ministries. Many will agree that it is a painful business to want to serve God through one's church, and to feel strongly called so to do, only to find that the very fact of wanting to is in itself regarded by those in authority as a nuisance.

In an effort to find a way round this difficulty and yet continue authentically in my own search, I have begun to think that it may in fact be necessary to take on the matter of being considered a nuisance as part of the road. Apart from any other considerations, this may make living with the situation less wearing – no mean aim in itself.

One matter which I have found helpful here is for me to grasp the fact that those in authority in the churches often suffer the same doubts and fears as many of the rest of us. If I can remind myself of this, then I think that it is probably possible to fell less suppressed, less depressed, by the apparent anomalies concerning women in ministry which surround some of us on a daily basis.

The first time I became aware that there might be another way to deal with the issue besides feeling bad about it and saying nothing, was more than thirty years ago, when caught up in the following incident – an incident which, although at the time I couldn't have named as a clever approach to speaking out against gender discrimination, I now see as precisely that. We were at choir practice, tackling a Bach Oratorio – no less! – and, at one point during the rehearsal, our gentle choirmaster read aloud the printed instructions on the score: 'The Disciples and the Holy Women,' said he, and he looked towards that section of the choir from whence he could reasonably have expected some sound to emanate. Before a note could be sung, however, a voice immediately behind me in the Alto section of the choir called out loud and clear, 'Why can't we be both?' There was a stunned silence – our choirmaster was not one to be challenged. Heads turned, and I saw behind me a beautiful young female face, smiling brightly at the choirmaster. 'What did you say?' he asked, looking perplexed. 'I said, why can't we be both?' came the reply, and the smile that accompanied her question was dazzling.

There was much laughter, but surely she had a succinct point. Why, indeed, was the word 'disciples' taken to apply only the men, and why was this exclusivity not questioned? I did not know then what I know now, that I was witnessing articulate feminism for the first time, and indeed I was also being shown a distinct way of taking on the task – vocation if you will – of educating others that many givens need questioning. For many of us the idea of questioning even a printed instruction on a musical score – that is, one which does not relate to the notes – was unthinkable, and still more the idea of questioning ecclesiastical structures. We were, quite simply, educated to acquiescence.

Thanks to such as that member of our choir, things have radically changed in all walks of life, and thank heavens for that! Many have come to realise that the actual questioning, the challenging, may well be part of the road. And once that is appreciated, the questions flow. The strain of asking them can be lessened too, I think, once we realise that there is nothing untoward in asking them in the first place – in fact, in the interest of truth, there may be no other way to go.

A couple of years ago, an eminent politician here at home decided to move to the back benches from a position of prominence. An interviewer on radio asked, 'What will you do now?' and the rejoinder came swiftly, 'I'll hang around and continue to make a nuisance of myself.' That particular decision has since been well proven to have been of benefit to us all.

Concerning women, therefore, in matters ecclesiastical, it seems to me now that, until truth and justice prevail, some of us might just as well take up this same course. It may well be that in this day and age a number of women and men are called to ask the awkward questions, and if that means being considered a nuisance by some others, what of it?

But we will need patience and tenacity, and some sense of humour also, I don't doubt. I have heard the theologian, Joan Chittister, OSB, suggest when speaking of those engaged in Christian Feminism that they will need to develop 'a theology of the long haul' and I am sure she is right. There are days, too, when one might wonder 'Why bother?' I ask it of myself betimes, and others – gently, but with a certain recognisable and understandable weariness, perhaps – ask it of me also. The answer, I suppose, is in something I once (to my delight) heard the head of the Dominicans, Timothy Radcliffe, say, and I hope, and venture to believe, that my memory serves me correctly as to his exact words, which were, 'Where (people) are locked in loving argument, there is God, because there is a deep search for the truth.'

It is from such belief that I take heart.

CHAPTER 1

Peeling back the layers

To say that we can possibly minister to the poor ... and
never read a single article on the national debt; to think
that we can possibly be moral parts of a global community and never study a thing about Third World debt; to
imagine that we can save the planet and never learn a
thing about ecology; to infer that we work to promote
the women's issue but never go to a women's conference, read a feminist theologian or spend a minute trac-
ing the history of ideas about women; to say we care
about the homeless dying and never say a thing about
the evil of homelessness or the lack of medical care for
the indigent, smacks of pallid conviction at best ... The
world needs thinkers who take thinking as a spiritual
discipline. Anything else may well be denial practised
in the name of religion.
            —Joan Chittister, OSB, *The Fire in These Ashes*

One of the most thought provoking conferences I have
ever attended took place in St Columban's, Dalgan Park,
Navan, Co Meath, in the Spring of 1994, and was given by
one Dr Brendan Lovett, himself a Columban, who for the
past twenty years and more has been serving on the mis-
sions in the Philippines. The title of the conference was
'Towards a Systematic Theology of Mission – Articulating
the Challenge'. It would probably take a whole book to
cover all the points he made, but such was the passion
with which he made them that he set me on a train of
thought which is with me still, and although I know that I

can only hope to touch on the breadth of his message, I hope that to do this is better than to do nothing.

Lovett believes (and he made it clear from the outset that much of his thought comes from the teachings of Bernard Lonergan, SJ, the author and theologian, who died in 1984) that the western world, including the churches, mistakenly believes that only we ourselves, on this part of the globe, know what it is to be human, and that it is this belief which is causing the systematic destruction of the planet Earth, and all life on it, including the human species. He also believes that as Christians we are under obligation to redress what he calls 'the suicidal path to self-destruction' on which we seem to be set. This was the belief of Lonergan also, who felt that as we come to the end of the twentieth century we are at the end of a long cycle of decline, and we must 'either respond creatively or wipe ourselves out'. Lonergan also insisted that 'what are least private to people are their insights. "My experience" does not exist in an individualistic sense. It can only be taken in relation to the genetic throbbing of history.'

This is a broad canvas, and, as I heard him at that conference, the salient points of Lovett's argument were:
  – that there is only one Story, one Mystery, one Universe, of which humanity is a part;
  – that the only way in which it is possible for us to live creatively in today's world is by taking a global viewpoint, and by having some understanding of the history of the universe from the beginning of time;
  – that, particularly in the past 500 years, 'humanity has misdefined what is humanly desirable', as a result of which we are literally cutting the very ground from under our own feet as we destroy rain forests, coral reefs, rivers, oceans and animal species, and even whole peoples, in the mistaken belief that this will bring about 'progress';

– that we are immersed in consumerism, to the detriment of all life;

– that it is essential that we learn to distinguish between living authentically and living inauthentically, and, following on that, essential that we cut out everything that is inauthentic in our way of life, both at a global and a personal, one-to-one level;

– that the only way to 'be church' today is to enter into the culture of the peoples with whom we live and to learn from them, since all imposition (of culture, etc.) is arrogant, wrong, and in the long run disastrous;

– that the church (the Roman Catholic Church) has gone along with what Lovett calls 'the aberration of the past 500 years' in imposing western culture on others;

– that we will only redress the situation when we stand with the oppressed and understand and name the damage we are inflicting on others and on the world by our destructive lifestyle.

With great skill, Lovett brought these points together, endeavouring to give direction as to how the gospel might be lived today. No stone was left unturned, nor were there any sacred cows. And it was here that I heard the statement, 'Unless we are prepared to peel back the layers of history, critiquing each one, any attempt to find a way forward will not stand up'.

As I heard this, I realised that everything he said could be applied to the matter of the authority church's attitude to the laity, and especially to women. Lovett's argument was that the church's attitude was basically flawed on many matters – for example, it went along with slavery. Imposition was the norm, rather than any effort to 'enter into'. Dialogue was never thought of as a way forward. Is not all of this true also with regard to what has happened between the authority church and women?

Lovett also believes that the western world, including the churches, look on people and things as resources, which in itself is totally wrong, because resource means 'that which will become valuable when we make something else of it', whereas all of creation has its worth simply because it *is*. We have lost sight of this, and the result has been cata-strophic damage worldwide.

It is Lovett's belief that it is imperative that we articulate what is wrong, and spell out how things could be other-wise. 'If we cannot name things, we cannot act.'

That is why I believe that it is necessary that, nuisance or not, those of us who feel the need to speak out about the ways in which certain matters are handled in the churches, with regard to the laity and especially to women, must do so. Lovett states that to do this 'we must start with our-selves, and understand what is going on in ourselves, and thus will we begin to understand why we (in this case the church) are as we are. Only then will we be able to open up to the truth'. If we can do this, Lovett holds, we will begin to see that 'there is no privileged place to stand; wherever we are, we are part of the whole, and cannot claim to be the only truth, but one of several streams of humanity, all of which contain some truth'. Again, I see this being equal-ly true with regard to the world, the churches, and women. Only if we can grasp the fact that every human is equal to every other, can we follow the truly human way of being. And the only way to do this is by dialoguing with all others, in all their varied richness.

One of Lovett's closing comments was that 'you cannot get at the meaning of the scriptures standing no place. We must dialogue with people "where they are", and this is what we have failed to do in the immediate past.' Strong words, and yet how true with regard to the authority church's attitude to the laity, and particularly women!

And he points out that as Christians we can look to Jesus, who fully embraced his own human life, living it to the full, with all its necessary limitations. In the humanity of Jesus we learn what it is to be human, and from this we can move forward in a life-giving way, by what Lovett calls, 'the mysterious law of the cross'. To stand with fellow humans in their poverty must take priority over all else. 'We must help people into the driving seat. The power must never be taken away from people, since nobody knows better than they what is best for them.'

How does that sound in relation to the church's dealings with women? And yet he points out that what is needed is change in structure, to allow for conversion, since to push someone into a position simply means that that person does not get there validly. And this, of course, poses a dilemma for all lay people, and especially for women: if the authorities in the churches do not come to the belief that all are fully human and fully spiritual, then for rules to be changed (say, to allow for the ordination of women in the Roman Catholic Church), before this belief had been reached, would be inauthentic. Change (conversion) is always gift. Waiting (in this case for others) to receive that gift can be both troublesome and tiring! And the only thing I have come up with is that we must at least help those others towards disposing themselves to readiness to receive the gift when it is offered – as one fine day it surely must be!

It would seem, then, that the task which faces us all is the task of stripping back the layers. It is probably true to say that to do so at any level is going to cause pain – part of which, of course, is the pain we feel at the thought that perhaps if we keep stripping back we will find nothing in the centre, like an onion... Yet there seems no other way forward, and therefore I believe that we must take that chance in faith.

CHAPTER 2

The women who walked with Jesus

And there were many other women there who had come
up to Jerusalem with him (Mk 15:41).

One obvious place to start peeling back, as I see it, is to
look at the relationships Jesus had with the women whom
he encountered during his public life. We can, I believe, be
sure that these stories must have held great significance
then, as they do for many now, because they were recorded
in such detail – even though they were stories involving
women, who counted for so little at that time.

The chances are that, in the eyes of the then authorities, the
women who were close to Jesus were seen as wretched
nuisances, every woman Jill of them. Better still, Jesus
himself, in these relationships, as he upended all the pre-
vailing rules, conventions and traditions, was no doubt
also considered a confounded nuisance by those same authorities because he gave importance to those relationships. I find this useful to remember; it gives me heart.

Call to ministry
Generally, when I think of the women who knew Jesus, the
first to come to my mind is the woman at the well. This
marvellous story is remarkable on several levels, and not
least because nowhere else in the gospels is there recorded
such a long conversation between Jesus and just one other.
That she was a woman, and a Samaritan at that, adds to its

uniqueness. He broke every taboo when he engaged her in conversion. And I find the dialogue between them intensely moving, partly, I think, because of the complete lack of small talk. How wonderfully direct they both are! No issues dodged, no punches pulled – on either side. And yet, in spite of this extraordinary honesty (or perhaps because of it?) there is also, as I hear it, a real gentleness, even a tenderness, in their exchange.

Surely when that woman – nameless, since as a woman she did not warrant being named – 'left her jar' and went to 'tell the others', she was responding to a call by Jesus to direct ministry. How else could she have faced all those people, who only a short while earlier she had been avoiding by coming to the well at a time when there would be no-one else around? And are we not clearly told that 'many believed, because of her testimony'? If we cannot call this a response to a call to direct ministry, what can we call it? I cannot think of another name for it.

I am sure, too, that when the disciples came looking for Jesus and registered surprise at finding him engaged in conversation with her, they certainly would have considered her a nuisance – although it has always intrigued me that they 'said nothing'. Did they know better than to question him, I wonder?

So, how did it come about, at a later stage in the history of the church, that women were forbidden to spread the word? Who decided this new arrangement? Surely if we (the church) had followed Jesus' example, women would still be preaching, just as the Samaritan women did? It must have taken a deliberate effort on the part of some people, at a later date, to rule this out of order.

Edwina Gately, the British lay worker, deals wonderfully with this subject. She says, on one of her very amusing – and very clever, and very relevant – tapes that, when St

Paul declared that women mustn't preach in church, this was because at that time they actually *were* preaching, but that one day the Patriarchs, as she puts it, 'woke up, decided they'd had enough of listening to the women, went into the churches and said, "Good morning Ladies. New rule: none of you is allowed to speak in here from now on. That's it! Silence, please! Off you go home; we'll take care of the preaching, thank you!"' Patriarchy at its most patriarchal – and most patronising! And maybe Edwina Gately is right. Maybe that's exactly what did happen. At the very least, it might behove those who insist that women must not speak in church today to study the matter more closely in order to try to make a better case for themselves, so that those of us who don't understand how the rule came about might perhaps be persuaded. Might.

Persistence

Then, there is the story of the woman who had been haemorrhaging for twelve years. This is a great story of persistence. (Nothing wrong with that). For all of those years this woman must have lived a life of complete seclusion, since she would have been considered unclean by everyone else because she was bleeding. No-one would have eaten with her, touched anything she used, touched her. And yet it seems that somehow she heard about Jesus and felt that if she could just get near him, something might happen to improve her lot. I imagine that her journey to find him must have been a very frightening one for her. She probably covered her face, so that no-one would recognise her. And she must have had to push her way through the crowd which at that time surrounded him, afraid that at any moment she would be recognised. And there must have been fear in her heart too as to how he would greet her. But her persistence and her courage paid off. And this, I find, makes the story an immensely encouraging one for the rest of us. It seems to me to underline the fact that there may well be times when stubborn faith and equally stubborn persistence are the only ways to make a point. And sometimes I think that women in particular – and sometimes particular women – have quite a capacity to be persistent. Perhaps, too, the quality of patience, which many women have, is compatible with that of persistence.

In fact, that woman took a great chance, because we know by Jesus' reaction to her when he felt her touching him that she had run the risk of being considered a nuisance by him also; yet her faith carried the day.

Sometimes I think that women may have learned, through millennia of having to suffer patriarchy, that persistence and patience are necessary in the search for ways forward for them. However, it does seem a crying shame that so much of women's energy has to be spent in this kind of struggle when it might be put to use in more positive ways.

Not many months ago, the editor of a periodical asked me if I would write something for him on preaching. The moment I tried to put pen to paper I realised that I could write from one perspective only, that of the listener. I realised that 99.9% of all preaching (in my own church) is done by men. This means that there is almost never a homily or sermon in my church which gives a woman's viewpoint on any of the readings throughout the entire year. How extraordinarily unbalanced! And what a waste! Think of all the excellent women teachers who can put their point succinctly in the classroom, for example. Why on earth can the church authorities not see the foolishness of barring such women and others from speaking in church? There is simply no logic here.

It is one of the wonders and mysteries of life, I think, that despite the negativity towards women in the Christian churches, some have managed to speak their minds. Julian of Norwich had things to say and said them, as did Teresa of Avila. And the intrepid Catherine of Siena counselled popes – even when they wished she wouldn't. But these are only a handful. It is hard to imagine how many opportunities must have been lost over the past two thousand years because women could not take part in a full way in church teaching. And what a different church we might have today if they had!

Courage and compassion

Another woman who has for centuries been part of the tradition of the story of Jesus, although she is not mentioned in the gospels, is Veronica. To me, this legend depicts a woman of outstanding courage and compassion, stepping forward out of the noisy crowd to wipe his face – the only comfort she could hope to give him at that moment. In this story, no doubt there were many who found her a great nuisance, as she slowed them down in their task of getting the broken man to carry his own instrument of death up the hill. Legendary though she may be, her story has been an inspiration to many, over many centuries.

Jesus' understanding of womanhood

Mary of Magdala is no legendary figure, but a real-life person, and an integral part of the story of Jesus. When I remember her, I usually like to think of her on the day when she went to the tomb to anoint his body. This must have been one of the loneliest journeys she had ever made. Many of us know what it is like to slip back into a room to sit for a few moments beside the body of a loved one who has just died. It is a lonely place to be. And yet we sometimes find it necessary to make such a journey; it is as if there is a need to do 'just one last thing' for the loved one.

And surely we must take heart from the fact that it was at this moment that Jesus chose to appear to her – and that he chose her above everyone else to appear to first – this woman who may well have been someone who through-out her life had loved 'not wisely, but too well'. I believe Jesus understood Mary's love for him, would have known not only of the greatness and depth of that love and would therefore have wanted to ease her pain, but also that he in turn loved her in such a way that it was natural for him to seek her out first.

One of the reasons why I believe that the love between these two was great, and that they had such an under-standing of each other, was because of the fact that she recognised him when he pronounced her name. Can we not all relate to this? Are there not people in our own lives who speak our names in such a way that we know that it can be no other who addresses us? And do we not some-times know also, by the very intonation of that voice, that we are loved?

Jesus must have been the most sensitive of human beings; I believe that this story of his meeting with Mary of Magdala tells us much, not only of their relationship with one another, but also of his understanding of womanhood. The story rings true for me.

The power to anoint

And this puts me in mind again of the story of the woman whose love for Jesus gave her the strength and the courage to do what seemed right to her at the time, she who poured the precious oil over his head. He said that we would talk about her for ever. And so we do. What an ex-traordinary story this is – and not just for women. What an extraordinary story it is for the authorities in the church! Again, on studying his words, the questions will not go away. If, as he said, she had the power to anoint him, then who subsequently took that power away from women? And when? And to what purpose? We must keep asking.

I believe that there is no such thing as an illegitimate quest-ion. Every 'why', every 'why not' is valid, in the interests of truth and justice.

Moreover, not only are the questions valid, but it is vital that they be asked, and we must allow no-one to tell us otherwise. And if we cannot get satisfactory answers, then I believe that we must question the validity of the rule-making.

Loyal opposition

And what of the two sisters, Mary and Martha? We are told with no ambiguity whatever that Jesus loved both of them – and this love was undoubtedly reciprocated. Their story draws for us a wonderful picture of two disparate women, each loving in her own way: Martha, unable to be still when there are things to be done, and Mary, the reflec-tive one; each loving him as only she could.

And as to what is commonly considered Jesus' reprimand to Martha for fussing, well, is it not possible that he might simply have been regretting out loud that practical things had to be done, as many of us do when we must get on with something although we might much prefer to sit down and talk? I feel that there is a good possibility that this was the case – and also that he may have realised that Mary needed time to talk to him, and that Martha facilitated this.

I also believe that when Jesus said that Mary had chosen the better part he merely meant that she had chosen the better part *for her*. He knew Martha too well to expect her to sit quietly. Each to her own. Jesus was not going to repri-mand Martha for being Martha. All that any of us is ever asked to do is to be ourselves.

As to the fact that both of these women in turn reprimanded him for not coming sooner on the death of their beloved

brother, it is my belief that these reprimands must have hit
Jesus hard at the time, because I believe that he himself
was so devastated at the death of his friend that he needed
time to himself before facing the women's grief. Their grief
would, I think, have compounded his own, and I don't
think he felt ready for that. And yet the fact that they could
reprimand him gives me heart because it clearly shows, as
I see it, that they both knew that they could reprimand him
without fear of jeopardising their friendship with him, or
losing his love.

And surely this is friendship at its best. It strikes me also
that that is how things should be between the ordinary
members of the church and the authority members. It
should be possible to express what the late Joe Dunn
called 'loyal opposition', without fear of being ostracised.

Anyhow, that is how I like to interpret that particular story
of Martha and Mary, and their individual and very different relationships with Jesus.

The steadfast mother

I suppose it's reasonable to assume that of all the women
who knew him, the one who must have known him best
was his mother. Mary was undoubtedly a strong woman,
even when she was young. How else could she have responded as she did to such a preposterous request as was
made of her? There is also, however, as I see it, great encouragement to those of us who may sometimes be lab-
elled troublesome by our questioning, in the knowledge
that Mary did not agree to become the mother of God until
she had asked some questions first. I am always glad to remind myself of this when I feel the need to persist with a
particular line of questioning. Only when Mary had received some replies – however enigmatic those replies
may have been – did she say yes, the yes on which so
much depended.

And, like anyone who says yes to anything, she can have had no idea at that moment just what she was letting herself in for. She had to take a leap of faith – something which all of us have to do, I think, not just once, but many times, perhaps even throughout one day. For Mary it can have been no easier than for anyone else. She was a young girl; she was going to have to face opposition and disapproval from all sides – from her parents, her fiance, the neighbours, and without doubt the Establishment. It must have taken courage to say yes then, as it often does now.

We know practically nothing of the thirty years which Jesus and Mary spent together. But we are free to imagine. Almost all that we are told is that Mary 'pondered'. And she surely had much to ponder. She can only have been learning as she went along, like the rest of us. Could she have had any inkling about who her child actually was? At best, I think it can only have been inkling, since I believe that, being fully human, he himself would have had to wait until his last breath before he knew the whole truth himself. No doubt she knew that he was 'different'. But how much else did she know?

I am sure that there were moments of great love between these two during those private years. Surely, too, there must have been moments of exasperation! What mother could truthfully say that at no time did an offspring manage to go through childhood, adolescence and early adulthood without some differences of opinion arising during the course of ordinary everyday living! The generation gap hardly started with this century!

Even the story of the wedding feast at Cana gives us some idea of their different ways of going about things. Jesus didn't take kindly, it seems, to being told by his mother that their hosts were embarrassed. In his book, *The Gift of Feeling*, the writer, psychologist and Medical Practitioner,

Paul Tournier, has taken up this very point. He believes that this incident may well have been the moment at which Jesus learned that his private life was coming to an end and his public life had to begin. Tournier speculates that it may have fallen to Mary to point this out to him, because as a woman she intuitively understood this before Jesus himself did.

No doubt this could be argued, but I find it an interesting point of view. And the very fact that Jesus responded so unenthusiastically to Mary's 'interference' will surely resonate with many parents! Nothing new here!

Neither do we know for just how many of those years Joseph was alive, and at what age Jesus would have had to take over the role of provider. But again, we are free to imagine. We know that it takes courage and strength to bring up a child single-handedly. No doubt Mary's strength and belief saw her through many an everyday domestic difficulty.

Outside Salisbury Cathedral in the south of England there is a beautiful sculpture called 'The Walking Madonna', by Elizabeth Frink. It is remarkable not least because it is not, like most statues, up on a plinth, but is set in the grass, so that Mary is, as it were, walking with everyone else. The statue is slightly bigger than life-size and it depicts a woman of later years; she has a deeply lined face, a face which tells of human suffering. And, also most interestingly, she is walking *away* from the Cathedral, as if to suggest that she has been in there, has prayed, and is now setting out to do whatever work is ahead of her in the course of her ordinary day. I find it an inspiring sculpture, and very different to any other image of Mary that I have come across.

In Dublin, in the Spring of 1996, there was an exhibition of art work by some women sculptors and artists, and among the exhibits was the original full-size cartoon, or line drawing, of this very sculpture. It showed the back view of the figure, a figure of strong, vibrant movement, as Mary strides along, with lovely flowing lines of torso and limbs. From this drawing, as from the finished sculpture, there seems to exude a wonderful energy. It is a completely unsentimental depiction of Mary, and I like to believe that Elizabeth Frink may have got it just right.

And no doubt that same strength stood to Mary when it came to the misery of Calvary. No doubt also but that Jesus knew that Mary would be there right to the end – you learn about people's strengths and weaknesses if you live with them long enough. He himself would have been aware, I am sure, of just who had gone the distance with him, but many others must have learned at the foot of the cross that it was some of his women friends who remained steadfast, and who didn't run away.

Surely from this it would have been logical for the early Christian Church to have followed his example, accepting women into ministry at every level.

There are some historians who believe just that – that the early Church did have women fully involved, and that not until some time later did patriarchy get into its stride, cutting women out of full participation. Joan Chittister says we are paying the price ever since. I'm sure she's right.

CHAPTER 3

The church authorities, women and ministry

The church cannot pretend that it is committed to justice and at the same time ignore the way that women are discriminated against, especially if the institutional church itself is one of the perpetrators. There is also no doubt that many women experience great pain and a sense of exclusion at the way they are treated by the church. The response of many churchmen is to say that these women have no good reason to feel pain, that their reaction is irrational, that the church can do nothing about it, and so on. Yet one suspects that if men were to express such pain, then the institutional church would sit up and take notice.

– *Women in the church – An issue of solidarity,* by Lennon, O'Hanlon, Toner and Sammon, (Jesuit Centre for Faith and Justice, 1995)

One of the statements made by the theologian Brendan Lovett, during the conference to which I referred at the beginning of this book, concerns the need to 'help people into the driving seat, since only they know what is best for them'. And this, obviously, has implications for more than the people about whom he was speaking at that time, the people of the so-called Third World; it has clear implications for women in the church and the church's attitude to women. Helping women into the driving seat was precisely what Jesus did for those women whom he encountered who were in some way deprived of the freedom to be in charge of their own lives. He gave them new strength.

The Ordination of women to the priesthood

In March 1995 about three hundred people, women, men, some ordained, some single, some married, and some from churches other than the Roman Catholic, gathered at a meeting in Dublin organised by B.A.S.I.C – Brothers and Sisters in Christ – a movement for the promotion of ordination to the full priesthood of women in the Roman Catholic Church. And one of the most remarkable things about the gathering, to this participant, was the lack of anger. It has often been otherwise when many women, and sometimes with men alongside them, attend such meetings. But on this occasion there was a notable absence of anger, which made the atmosphere unique.

We listened to an ordained woman from the Church of Ireland who spoke of her own and others' solidarity with us, and she said that this solidarity was in itself a source of joy to her. And the more I listened, the more I became convinced that it will be women who will bring about the healing of division among the Christian churches.

The main speaker at the conference was Professor Mary McAleese, Vice-Chancellor of Queen's University, Belfast. She pulled no punches when she spoke of the need for the powers that be in our church to begin to heed the movement for the ordination of women which now exists within the body of the church. She drew attention to the fact that, since there are no official channels through which women may speak to those in authority (although this is slowly changing), the body of well-informed, articulate women who now exist within the church membership still find it necessary to give voice to their opinions and insights 'by shouting, from the outside'. It is a ludicrous picture, especially in a church which purports to cherish all its members equally.

Three women at the conference spoke of their felt call to

the ordained priesthood, and one described the rejection of her vocation to full priesthood twenty years ago as feeling like 'an abortion of a child of God'. And she then told a hushed room that when, twenty years on, the call had come back even more strongly, it was as if she had discovered that 'the child had not in fact died, but was alive and kicking'. It was a most moving account of an unfulfilled vocation.

One grandmother told us that her own daughter had recently had great difficulty in taking her newly-born son to the church for baptism, because she felt she was having her son 'baptised into a church which denigrates his mother, his grandmother and his sisters'. In the event, she decided to 'make an act of faith', and allow the ceremony to proceed.

A priest spoke of the pain he has always felt, before, during and since his ordination, because he is so acutely aware of the injustices perpetrated on women by the church into which he has been ordained, and he too said that he was having to work 'through faith'.

At the end of the day, one – ordained – said to me, 'We are at peace today here because it's so obvious; it quite simply has to come.' I think he was right. There would be so much offered by women in full ministry, because, by and large, women have a different way of being from men.

What difference would it make?

I often think that because many women are very close to the experience of birth and of death they know a significant amount about ministry; they are at the coal face, and it is mostly they who do the bulk of the caring, at least in this part of the world. Most women's respect for life is enormous. After all, if you have given birth, you know the price paid, and I believe that few women would wish, for instance, to draw up battle lines for wars. Pregnancy, birth, and years of nurturing make a person aware of the need to preserve life, aware of the preciousness of life. And I often wonder, when I see on the TV screen row upon row of grey-suited men sitting down to discuss strategy concerning worldwide friction, as to whether if even half of those present were women, the strategy might not be different, at least on occasion.

I wonder about this also when I see the rows of splendidly garbed members of the hierarchy and College of Cardinals parading into their very important meetings – meetings at which no doubt will be discussed, amongst other things, matters which directly concern women. It is highly unlikely that a woman will be there to give women's points of view. No-one will be there to explain, for example, in a discussion on family planning, the day-to-day problems of a family which is too big for any one woman to cope with; no-one will be there to explain the pain of repeated sexual violence resulting in repeated pregnancies; no-one will be there to explain what it is like to be totally financially dependant on someone who drinks all the income, leaving nothing with which to feed and clothe a family; in other words, no-one will be there to tell it as it is in the real world of many women.

Liturgies would be different if women were more involved. I recently received an invitation to attend a conference on Mission in Asia, and it is undoubtedly true that for me one of the highlights of that conference was the communal worship by people of different religions which took place at the end of the first day. The room set aside for this worship ('we have created a space' is how one described it) was furnished minimally, with only a beautiful arrangement of flower petals painstakingly set out in the centre of the floor, and many small candles placed around the room. The bible rested on a low stand on the floor, and around the walls were large cushions, the only seating. And all of this was organised by women participants. The gentle light from the candles, the lack of clutter, and something about the informality of the seating appeared to me to create an ambience of tangible silence. There were perhaps eighty people present, and yet that silence remained undisturbed – curiously, it seemed to do so even when we prayed aloud by quiet chanting or singing. Sometimes we prayed by a gentle dance movement, in which everyone who wished could join. But much of the time the silence was total. And everything, as I saw it, from the arrangement of the flower petals to the varying forms of prayer, appeared to be in rounded or circular form.

I have no hesitation in saying that the lack of hierarchical structure, the lack of straight lines, the lack of a 'them up there, us down here' atmosphere, made this a liturgy in which I felt myself to be wholly included – not something which I can say about most liturgies I attend.

How long this liturgy took I cannot say, because time was not of the essence. Of the essence were the reflective atmosphere, the complete lack of disturbance or intrusion or aggression, the sense of unity and, as I experienced it, some sense also of an understanding by all present of the place of humanity in the whole of creation, as we joined with that creation in worshipping the One. I found myself asking: is this not the essence of prayer?

There is need, too, to talk about the breaking of the bread. One of the difficulties facing those who would wish to maintain the status quo is that there are many who are prepared to argue against the belief that when Jesus said 'Do this in memory of me' he was addressing men only – or they might argue that even if he did, this was because of the historical position of women at the time. Many are beginning to question the accepted interpretation of who it was that Jesus so instructed. It is very hard indeed to believe that, at the time when he lived, no woman would have presided at a table in a house where he sat down for a meal. We have contrary evidence, in fact, in the story of Mary and Martha. And it is very hard to see why this should have changed after his death – except that at some later stage some people made a definite decision to set up the prohibition which now stops women from presiding at a eucharistic table.

Sometimes I wonder what shape such a meal might have taken, if women had had input over the forming years. Once I heard a woman comment on our present day experience of eucharist, and she said 'Can you imagine any woman serving herself before serving the others at her table?' I experienced something even more inexplicable some time ago when I was asked by the organiser of a eucharist at a relatively small gathering if I would be a minister of the eucharist for the occasion. I hesitated, because I knew that the celebrant was not partial to shared ministry, but I was prevailed upon to agree. At the appropriate time I approached the altar. The celebrant raised the large host, then lowered it, broke it into four pieces – and consumed the four pieces himself! I could not help but wonder at that moment whether he had any understanding at all of the symbolism of breaking bread and sharing. I wondered what sort of training he had had through his years in the seminary, and I wished with all my heart that there had been women involved in this training, as well as men, women who know what it is to break and share bread on a daily basis in their own homes.

One-to-one ministry

Many women are extraordinarily good at one-to-one ministry, because of their own life experience. Many women care on an individual basis for their babies at the most vulnerable time of the babies' lives. Many of them also care for elderly relatives. I have seen extraordinary devotion between friends – particularly, it seems to me, between women friends – devotedly caring for one another, sometimes for as long as fifty or more years, and ministering to one another – although they might not use those words – in a way that I can only describe as awesome. And I cannot but think that this is the essence of ministry, in which is best reflected the love of the Creator for all creatures. There is something far less demanding in standing at a lectern and speaking to several hundred. The demands of one-to-one ministry, whether in a marriage or any other relationship, the putting up with the other's idiosyncrasies, vagaries and humours, surely manifest more than any other ministry the meaning of unconditional love. This can, of course, apply to men as to women, and I do not suggest otherwise, but why is the church impoverishing itself by not allowing the female half of its members to minister at every level? We are all the losers.

Another one-to-one situation where I believe we are all losing out because women cannot be involved at a sacramental level concerns the Sacrament of Reconciliation. I am increasingly aware of the huge anomaly which exists between women and men when it comes to the reception of this sacrament. For a man, when he goes to confess his faults he should have some reasonable assurance that the person who is listening to him will be able to understand in a real way what his problems are; but even if a woman's confessor is the most understanding of men, and even if he has the best will in the world, the woman knows that her confessor does not know what it is to be a woman, and it stands to reason that he therefore cannot fully understand the penitent's story, with all its nuances. This perception may be right or wrong, but it is very real for many women. And for that reason there can be no comparison drawn between the two situations of a man receiving the Sacrament

of Reconciliation, and a woman. Why should this difference be?

Women can, of course, and many do, talk to one another
about all that is most important to them – I think here of
Mary hurrying to share her news with Elizabeth. Many
women know full well the blessing it is to have a female
friend with whom it is possible to discuss everything. I
know too that many women, and some men also, find it
possible to discuss all sorts of things with their friends of
the opposite sex, but I am equally sure that there are times
when I myself will want to share something with a woman
friend. Why is sacramental absolution not possible, in
such circumstances? And how can this further anomaly
exist in a church which calls itself Christian?

Not long ago, in a letter to *The Tablet*, the editor of *Studies*,
Rev Noel Barber, SJ, said '... if one asserts that it is the will
of God that women be excluded from Orders and so from
governance in the church, one is equivalently saying that it
is God's will that women be subject to men in the church'.
This seems to me to be the truth of the matter. It is only one
example, but enough in itself, I often think, to point up the
injustices with which women have to live, within the present patriarchal system. It makes a nonsense of calling our
church Christian in the true sense of the word, since Jesus
Christ went to such lengths to do away with the imbal-
ances which existed in the patriarchal establishments of
his day, in order that we might follow suit. Is it not time,
2,000 years on, that we tried a bit harder to emulate him?

The Ordination of ex-Anglican priests

Rules, and the keeping of them, brings me to a topic much
in the news in recent times, that of the Roman Catholic
Church accepting married Church of England priests into
its priesthood. In many cases it does seem that the priests
are converting precisely because the Roman Catholic

Church is not ordaining women. The fact that this is why they are moving from their own church and being received by mine seems appalling, and my church's acceptance of them equally appalling. I find it extraordinarily insulting to women.

I have before me a cutting from a weekly Catholic newspaper, on the front page of which there is a photograph of three smiling middle-aged men in full ecclesiastical dress. The man in the middle is a bishop of my own church, and the other two are ex-bishops of the Anglican Church. And, according to the write-up accompanying the photo, they have joined my church because their own is ordaining women. There is no ambiguity whatever in the written statement.

Now, I think it's worth just using our imaginations here for a moment. Suppose that someone with no knowledge at all of religion were to fall from the sky and pick up this newspaper, what conclusion could that person come to, on reading this report? As I see it, he or she could only come to one, and that is that these men, splendidly garbed in their long flowing robes – dresses? – were the leaders of a misogynist sect. What else could anyone possibly think? And why are so many missing this point so badly? Is it not clear just what this statement concerning the non-ordination of women is saying? And, most serious of all, is it not clear that to say this in the name of Jesus, he who did all in his human power to point to the full humanity and full spirituality of women, is to go against his teaching?

I was also appalled to learn, on a radio interview with an ex-Anglican married clergyman who had converted to Roman Catholicism, that it is a rule that on his acceptance into the full priesthood of my church he sign a paper stating that, should his wife predecease him, he will not remarry.

As a woman I find this utterly offensive. It sounded to me as if these men were being told 'We (the Roman Catholic Church) need your services, and because of this we will have to put up with the fact that at present you are consorting with a woman. But if she should die, then make sure you keep yourself from further contamination.' I find this rule shameful and sinful, particularly when it is being done in the name of Christ. And I have failed to find another way of interpreting it.

It has come to my notice recently that, strangely, there are a good number of clergy in my own church who are unaware of this particular rule, and this surprises me. Many have been shocked when I told them of it. I wonder if those who do feel shocked by the rule could find it in their hearts to speak out loud about it? We women need our own clergy to speak up.

As I see it, there can only be two possible explanations for the rule: either it has been made by misogynists or it is being done for financial reasons, that is, the church will not take responsibility for the families of clergy. Both reasons are grossly insulting to women and children.

And we can push this further: these men, who are being received into my church because they disapprove of the ordination of women in their own, have wives and children. But my own church has already 'lost' thousands of its own priests – and some bishops – precisely because those priests and bishops have wished to develop, or have developed, loving relationships with women. In many cases they, too, have wives and children. So we really do have to ask, What's going on here? Why one rule for some, and another for others? Has no-one an overall view? Can no-one stand back sufficiently to get an overall view?

As it happens, some of us *are* standing back sufficiently, because we're on the fringe. And nothing is clearer from here than that this mess, illogical and utterly unjust, simply cannot stand up.

Women and sexual morality

There is another point which raises its ugly head for me here in this very gloomy picture, and it concerns the statement which is constantly being made by the authority church that 'every sexual act must be open to the transmission of life'. As a married woman well beyond middle years, I know that this simply does not measure up to my lived experience of marriage, and the only reason why such a statement is still being made by the church authorities is because they are not listening to accounts of the lived experience of married women and men. One would be inclined to ask who, even among the church authorities today, now that we are supposed to have what is called a greater understanding of what marriage is, really believes that this rule is even logical? I would venture to say very few.

As a mother, I can think of few more heinous crimes than that of the abuse of a young person. However, as the mother of daughters I must add that, should a situation arise where such abuse led to the pregnancy of a young girl, then to my mind this compounds the heinousness infinitely. It cannot be true, therefore, to state 'every sexual act must be open to the transmission of life'. There are times when the very opposite is true.

Do those in authority not realise that statements like this don't stand up? And do they not see that it might behove them to sit down and listen to women's views of such statements? Until they do, they are failing to serve one half of the members of the church. For this reason, if for no other, it is imperative that women be brought into the decision-making processes of the Roman Catholic Church.

How can we bring about change?

I had an idea recently about how such listening might be brought about. It struck me that what is needed is direct contact between the decision-makers and women, over a sustained period. And I fell to imagining that perhaps three or four women, married and/or single, could offer to give a retreat for some members of the hierarchy, say four or five. Just suppose for a moment that the retreat were to be called 'The Ministry of Listening', and just suppose that a programme something like the one laid out below could be implemented over three, four or even eight days. It could run something like this:

8 a.m. Meditation, to be led by one of the retreat directors.

9 a.m Breakfast, to be prepared by the retreatants.

10 a.m. Scripture reading aloud by one of the women directors, followed by an account by her of a story in her own life which relates for her to the scripture story.

11 a.m. Coffee.

11.30 a.m. 'Group', i.e., one and a half hours of sitting quietly together, dealing with whatever might come up for anyone, and 'suffering' one another.

1 p.m. Lunch, to be organised by the retreatants.

2-4 p.m. Free.

4 p.m. Coffee.

4.30 p.m. Discussion by all on the morning's scripture reading and the story which followed it.

6 p.m. Liturgy. The sole responsibility to be taken by the retreat directors, to take the form of a eucharist, but leaving a great hole or gap in the middle of the liturgy to demonstrate how, as things stand today, a liturgy organised by women can never be complete, since it cannot include the consecration of the bread and wine.

7 p.m Supper, to be the responsibility of the retreatants.

I think that this reversal of roles, and the time spent together, might add greatly to the understanding of all, and that much might be learned therefrom. Above all, I believe that the retreatants might experience just what it is like to be unable to fully celebrate the eucharist sacramentally when a group of women is gathered together for prayer. Perhaps equally important, they might also learn what it is like to 'think theology' while peeling potatoes for a household – which is the lived experience of very many women theologians. A few days like the ones I have just suggested might lead to a fuller understanding on the part of the church authorities of what it feels like to be on the fringe.

Clericalism

We cannot underestimate the mindset of clericalism. The following story may be outrageous, but it is also, unfortunately, true. A friend of mine was attending a social function and at one point found herself in the company of four clerical gentlemen, all, she thought, in their mid-thirties to mid-forties, and all, she felt, somewhat conservative. She was therefore quite agreeably surprised – and even chided herself inwardly for being hasty in her judgement – when one of them said, 'I am sure that celibacy for clergy will have to go.' However, her surprise and pleasure were shortlived, because the speaker immediately added, without a trace of mischievousness, 'Celibacy for priests will have to go, because priests are finding it harder and harder to get housekeepers.' As if this were not enough on its own, to her horror she then saw all other three clerical figures nod their collective heads solemnly in agreement!

My friend is both articulate and explosive. I do believe that by the time she left their company each of those clerics had gained a better understanding of the meaning of patriarchy, of clericalism, and, if they had never heard of it before, would have gained at least a rudimentary insight into Christian Feminism.

I am fully aware that many clerics do not *set out* to fail to comprehend the feelings of women with regard to their exclusion from church matters. In his last book, *No Vipers in the Vatican* (Columba Press, 1996), the late and greatly missed Joe Dunn tells the story of how he, along with some other clerics, was a guest of the then Bishop of Kerry, Eamonn Casey, in the bishop's summer residence in Kerry some twenty years ago. Dunn says, 'I am almost sure there was an American cousin in the background' (this reference being to Annie Murphy, whom we now know to be the mother of Peter, whose father is Eamonn Casey.) It did not seem to strike Joe Dunn that there was anything peculiar about the fact that there was another visitor on holiday in the same house but 'in the background'. Surely plain courtesy, or the supposedly famous Irish hospitality, might have ensured that this other guest could have been included in the meals and the conversations of those clerical guests who were present in the house? What price table fellowship?

Of course it might validly be argued that for his own good reasons Eamonn Casey had in that instance arranged things in this way, but that is not my point. What astounded me is that the others in the house apparently never considered the possibility that this female guest might have sat down to table with them, and joined in their conversations. What an extraordinary way to behave!

Or is it? I have brought this up recently with a number of people who should perhaps have more knowledge of these things than I, and the comments I get are invariably the same: 'It was – is – the norm; a group of clerics in a household would never have thought of including a woman in their company and conversation.'

Again, I ask: what price table fellowship? And is it not extraordinary that we should all have accepted such a situation as 'the norm' – and that perhaps there are times when some of us still do? I wish I might have put this point to Joe Dunn himself, but sadly this was not to be.

And so I begin to wonder if we have moved on at all from the time of Mark 15:40: 'There were some women watching from a distance'? It would appear not to any great extent – and we are the poorer for that.

Signs of hope?

But perhaps there is some very slight sign of change, at least in some quarters. Even as I was gathering this chapter together, the Roman Catholic Churches of Scotland and England have been rocked by a scandal, much as the Casey scandal rocked the Irish church four years ago. In this instance, one of the Scottish Hierarchy had disappeared, and it was thought that he was 'in the company of a woman'.

Within a couple of days, the news broke that that same man had a fifteen-year-old son, living in the south of England with his mother. This, naturally, rocked the Scottish and English churches even further. But ironically it is from this very story that I have gleaned a little hope, which has come about in this way: it happened that I had just tuned into BBC television when the latest revelation came through, and the newscaster spoke to Cardinal Hume live on the telephone, in the hearing of the entire television audience. And the Cardinal said three things clearly and completely spontaneously: he said that he had only just learned the news; that he was deeply shocked and saddened; and then he said – and this is where my heart lifted – 'My heart goes out to the woman and to her son, Kevin'.

In these words I see a glimmer of hope, because a senior member of the church has responded in a human way to a

human tragedy, *and has got the priorities right*. When the
Bishop Casey scandal first erupted in Ireland, as I remember it – and I would love to think others remember differently – I waited in vain for a senior member of the church
authorities to express concern about the injustice done to
Annie Murphy and her son, Peter, who for nineteen years
had struggled with life while Peter's father denied both of
them. This, to me, was the kernel. But we heard discussions about finance; discussions on the scandal of preaching one set of rules whilst living another; discussion even
about the great good done during that particular episcopacy. But I cannot remember, at the beginning of the unfold-
ing of the story, any member of the upper echelons of the
church using words such as those used by Cardinal Hume
this time round – words which reflect so much more truly
those of Jesus who, we are told, was often 'moved to pity'.

On the list of priorities dealt with at the time of the Casey
scandal it appeared to me that concern for the two
wronged, vulnerable people came very far down indeed.
What a difference it would have made if the gut reaction of
someone in authority in the church at the time had been
'My heart goes out to the woman and the boy! We must see
that they are treated justly.' But years and years of clericalism had ensured that this was well nigh impossible. And
there's the rub.

And that is why I felt some relief, and some edification,
when I heard Cardinal Hume speak, while still in shock at
the revelations concerning the then Bishop of Argyll and
the Isles. Perhaps, after all, there is some room for hope.

I do understand that Eamonn Casey is, as is each of us, a
victim of his time. And I am acutely aware that a bishopric
had an immense importance in the lives of many of us as
we grew up. But it would be a good thing *now* if we could
see some evidence that the ministry of parenthood were

given the precedence to which it is entitled. It is a sorry system indeed if any of us, either collectively or individually, still believes that the ministry of an episcopacy should take precedence, for anyone, over one's duties and responsibilities to one's own flesh and blood. Until we place these matters in their right order we cannot, as church, even pretend to be acting justly towards women and children.

A last comment concerning the injustices perpetrated on women in my own church: not long ago there was in *The Tablet* a lovely tribute to the late Bishop of Liverpool, Derek Worlock, and one of the points made was that he had always, from childhood, wanted to be a priest. And it appears that when the time came for him to enter the seminary, some small problems existed, but every barrier was removed and every door opened, by everyone, to make sure that he could follow his call to the priesthood. And how right and fitting this proved to be.

However, we must also give ear to another story, the story of a young woman who from early childhood felt called to that same priesthood. And when the time came for her to leave school, every door was closed, every barrier kept in place, and nowhere over twenty years has she been able to find even a chink of light through which she can glimpse a way forward in her endeavours to follow her calling to the ordained ministry, which she believes is being made to her by the Holy Spirit.

We must ask again and again, why was the response of the church to these two people so completely different? And how is it that those in authority in the Roman Catholic Church can decide to listen to and help one candidate, and fail to listen to and help the other, on gender grounds? Where is the Christianity in that?

I believe that we cannot ask these questions often enough.

CHAPTER 4

One angle on the celibacy debate

... strangers we too often are. Those years in the seminary sow the seeds of later segregation. The relative seclusion of the presbytery may well repel rather than attract both the seeker and the stranger. Celibacy and clerical dress contribute further to the sense of 'separateness'. It seems to me now, looking back over the training we received, that priests of my vintage were better equipped for the ministry of 'doing things' for people, rather than for the pilgrim task of simply being with them on a common journey.

— Seamus Ryan, 'Are we busy about the right things?' *The Church in a New Ireland*, Seán MacRéamoinn, ed., (Columba Press, 1996).

In her book on the religious life, *The Fire in these Ashes*, the Benedictine theologian Joan Chittister asks the question again and again, 'What is religious life for?', and again and again she gives the answer, 'It is to give witness; to be a light shining in a world which has for the most part forgotten God.'

This is, I believe, an authentic definition. It is also one which can easily be lost sight of in today's world, which is often a fast moving, confusing one, where nothing seems to stand still for very long on any front, where values once held sacred have been overthrown and, because for many money has taken the place of God, expediency in the acquiring of riches overrides much that used to be considered valuable. It is hardly surprising, then, that the need to love another is so manifest. It is my belief that many hope that, if they find such a love, they may find the kind of stability which is probably missing at other levels in their lives.

And I feel I can understand this. To me, intimacy with another (and I am by no means talking exclusively here of physical, genital intimacy) is the greatest reflection there is of the love of God for God's own creation. I mean here intimacy at every level – of mind, heart and spirit, and sometimes, but not necessarily always, with a physical dimension also. Therefore it follows, I think, that to deny oneself such intimacy, even if this denial is only at one level, is to relinquish much, and is in itself often heroic.

I also believe that intimacy with another or others is a vital part of any life which aspires to its full human potential. In order to become a whole, loving person it is, I think, essential for those who have voluntarily decided to deny themselves intimacy with another at a physical, genital level that they will experience intimacy of mind and heart and spirit, if they are to really understand the depth of the love of God for God's own creation. And I sometimes wonder if everyone who leads a celibate life 'in religion' understands this fuller meaning of intimacy.

I wonder, because of some conversations I have had with some who are living truly exemplary lives in religious institutions and seem, on the face of it, to be fully in tune with what they have taken on by their commitment to celibacy. But, in each of the three instances cited below, I have been puzzled by some of the views I have heard expressed.

In one case, a theologian in the course of a lecture said, 'The Roman Catholic Church is, by demanding celibacy for its priests, asking that only those who love life so fully

that they do not need anything more put themselves forward
for the ordained priesthood.' (My italics). Somehow this
seems to me to imply possession, and at its most ideal I do
not see intimacy of body, mind or heart as having anything
to do with possession, but rather with mutuality. (In fact,
in the above case I believe that the lecturer left out a very
important point, about which there is much more in this
book elsewhere, in that he failed to mention that the
church may well be asking all that he states, but it is also
asking something else, and that is that the person applying
be male, and therein lies the absurdity, because there may
well be many thousands who 'love life sufficiently that
they don't need anything more' – but they may not be
male).

Leaving that digression aside for a moment – although it is
vitally important – I was also disturbed when I heard a
priest say on radio in an interview, which was by any stan-
dards both reasonable and gentle, in response to a question as to whether he had ever wished that he might have
experienced intimacy with a woman at a physical level,
that yes, he did wish he had, 'because I love life so much in
all its facets that I would like to have experienced that facet
of it as well, even once; but I know that there can never be
a case of "just once"'. It seemed to me that he was separating physical intimacy from other intimacies, and I found
this hard to take on board. Possibly there are those who
will say that this is one of the great differences in the way
in which men and women love, but I wonder how many
women or men would be able to talk about physical love
(at its most ideal, that is) without seeing it as part of a deep
friendship, rather than as something separate. And I wondered, because of this comment of his, if he really knew
what it is for non-celibate people to love at a physical level;
if he understood that in an ideal situation there would
need to be love at a myriad other levels also. Again, I re-

alise that I am speaking of the ideal, but nonetheless I believe that it is of vital importance that this be understood when one is defining physical intimacy as part of loving.

My third example concerns a most moving discussion I had with a celibate man, living an exemplary life in a religious order, who told me of the great and terrible loneliness many experience from time to time in such institutions. He mentioned that there were occasions when he himself wished that he might 'close the door and have some peace and ease and love, for once'. This simple statement seemed so truthful that I was greatly moved by it, but then he added that he was 'not talking about a sort of "quick fix" or anything like that', and these words startled me, causing me to wonder if he really believed that those of us who lead non-celibate lives live out our relationships at a physical level as some sort of facile solution, to be used at a whim. To denigrate physical intimacy thus would appear to me to mean that married – or other – partners would simply be reducing their relationships to the state of making use of one another, and I cannot for a moment agree that this is what love expressed in physical intimacy is about.

And so I fell to wondering as to whether, if this gentle, celibate man with whom I was in conversation has such a view of the physical intimate side of the lives of those who live 'out in the world', how many more celibates think as he does? Does not the very fact that even *one* can have such a view of non-celibate life point up the great gulf in understanding that exists between those who embrace celibacy and those who live intimately with another? And is this lack of understanding not something to be attended to, if we are ever to be able to minister to one another? Does it not point up the real need for dialogue, so that mutual understanding can be reached?

I would push this subject further, and say that I believe that there are many who live full intimate lives with another but who also live blameless lives insofar as other friendships are concerned, friendships which involve intimacy of mind and heart and spirit but which acknowledge boundaries and observe them. Loving friendships which achieve such mutuality can, I believe, be a most enriching part of life, whether one is celibate or not; there are delineations within which all of us must live. But it is my firm belief that friendship and love mirror best the love of God for us, and to forego such friendships for any reason is surely to impoverish oneself greatly and to miss the opportunity of understanding even more deeply the depth of the love of God for God's creation.

I am convinced that the need for men and women to know one another cannot be sufficiently stressed, and I believe that this is as true for celibates as it is for others. I was listening recently to John B. Keane being interviewed on radio about his play, *The Field*, and particularly about the main character, the awful, very frightening, very real, Bull McCabe. The interviewer commented that here was a 'really awful man, the worst kind imaginable' and, to the surprise of the interviewer as well as to this listener, and I should imagine many others, John B. replied, in a wonderful defence of the character he himself had created: 'But you must understand; it was his life that made him as he was; look, if, at any stage during his life he had felt a feminine hand on his shoulder, who knows what a different person he might have turned out?' I felt this to be a wonderfully expressed acknowledgement of just how important men and women are to each other on life's journey, if we wish to become whole, made in the image of our Creator.

A friend of mine with an interest in these things said to me recently, 'There is no shortage of vocations to the priesthood; there is a shortage of vocations to celibacy'. I think he is right. Especially during the past few decades, this message appears to be foremost in the minds of many. Those priests who leave their ministries to marry often express profound regret that they must cease to minister, and many of the women who are telling the authority church that they feel called to the ordained priesthood are themselves married.

It also seems clear – because of falling numbers in traditional vocations, and because of the admission of married men from the Anglican Church to the priesthood of my own church, to name but two reasons – that compulsory celibacy will soon disappear, but I have a real fear that it may do so for the wrong reasons. Here I know I plough a somewhat lonely furrow, when I wonder aloud if the present debate on whether or not ordained priests in my own church should be allowed to marry is the debate which should be taking place just now. I think it is the wrong debate. I would much prefer to see women being admitted to full ordained ministry at least at the same time as the ban on marriage for diocesan priests is removed, because I am fearful that, given my church's track record concerning its treatment of women, if the removing of the celibacy rule comes before the admission of women to full priesthood, women will still be seen as subservient. If, on the other hand, the debate concerned both men and women priests, then it would seem to me that it would be a much more valid debate, and, indeed, that others would then enter into it with more enthusiasm.

To put it at its most stark and uncomfortable: might it not be possible that the call for the abolition of the celibacy rule for diocesan priests might just compound the church's present attitude of seeing women simply as useful objects? Might they not, once more, be seen merely as a facility? I do not see this as beyond the bounds of possibility at all. Perhaps my doubts could be summed up thus: in this part of the world, although there has undoubtedly been some progress, gender equality is still quite hard to come by in any field. What chance equality within a marriage of two Roman Catholics where either or both partners might wish to serve their church in ordained ministry but only one is eligible, on gender grounds? Small, I fear, and for this reason I greatly wish that today's debate on priestly celibacy might give way to a debate on the real injustice, that of treating women as unworthy of answering the call which many of them feel, to be other Christs, just as their brothers feel that call. And where stands the church's protestations that by baptism all are called to the common priesthood? Again, nothing rings true.

I would, therefore, much prefer to see this injustice removed before the matter of optional celibacy for today's priests is dealt with, because if things were done in this order the debate would encompass everyone, and not just half the members of the church.

There is another serious point here which troubles me as a woman, and a married one, and that is that, despite all the clerical protestations to the contrary in recent years, I believe that there are many in our church, lay as well as clerical, who still feel that, somehow or other, a celibate life is in some way 'on a higher plain' than the life of a non-celibate. In spite of all the genuine efforts which have been made recently to speak of the sanctity of marriage, I believe that there is still a residue within the church authorities, and amongst the laity as well as the clerical members, who believe that both ways of life are not 'equal in sanctity.' (What an extraordinary phrase!) I wonder, therefore, if the constant emphasis on priestly celibacy does not, precisely because of the emphasis, devalue the lives of those whose vocation is different? It often seems to me that this is the case, and that the church authorities, by constantly hammering home the message that celibacy is a vital part of the call to full priesthood, thereby denigrates the lives of all others. It also means, of course, that no woman can ever, in the eyes of a church which insists on male celibacy for its priests, be other than 'second class'. None of this is helpful to lay people, and to women in particular.

We can also see full well from the lives of those in other Christian churches that a married clergy can minister with just as much understanding and compassion – some would say with perhaps even greater understanding and compassion – as those who are not living intimate family lives.

And so perhaps all of this begs the following questions: why not married priests, single priests, male priests, female priests; full-time priests, part-time priests, and priests for a committed number of years – perhaps ten, or twenty, and renewable or with the option of retiring? It would seem from all the evidence before us today that, no matter how tardily it will come about, in such thinking our best hope lies. Surely the sooner this is grasped by the authorities the better, so that there may yet be, as Joan Chittister says, still fire in the ashes of those 'in religion' today, from which new vocations may take flame.

CHAPTER 5

Lay Ministry: an obvious answer

There is a common expression of the need for a new prophetic ministry which will read the signs of the times with an unblinkered eye, and will proclaim the truth with clarity and courage ... a ministry in counter-point to, but preferably not in conflict with, that of priesthood.
— Seán MacRéamoinn, ed., *The Church in a New Ireland*, (Columba Press, 1996).

You wouldn't know where to begin. There is so much out of kilter concerning the manner with which the church authorities are dealing, or failing to deal, with the issue of lay ministry today that it's hard to prioritise the problems. It seems reasonable for me, however, to try to make a start on this subject about which I ought to know something, since I am both lay and interested in full-time ministry in the church.

I believe there is a need to discuss lay ministry on at least two practical levels: firstly, how will lay people be facilitated to use their gifts and answer their call to ministry, and secondly, how will their involvement, when it comes – as come it surely must – be funded?

I often wonder if anyone 'at the top' is working on these two questions. Concerning the latter, we have here at home numerous examples of people, often women members of Religious Orders, who work in the church and receive no remuneration. But that, as the number in religious orders declines, will end. Who is ready to grasp the nettle – as no doubt some see it – that lay people must be involved and that for this to happen they will have to be paid?

With regard to facilitating lay people at a deep level in mission and ministry, there is some movement in some quarters towards this, and I have been heartened over the past couple of years to learn that certain religious societies and orders are inviting lay people to join them in their work. One I have some experience of in this regard is the Society of St Columban, which invites lay people to join its members on mission for a period of three or more years, preceded by a training period. I see this move as most timely, and it seems to me to be one clear way forward.

The matter of remuneration is, I believe, a far greater problem, because for far too long we in Ireland have accepted the extraordinary work done by various members of religious institutions, for which we did not pay. Now, as vocations dwindle, there is a noticeable dearth of such people. Now, lay people are needed to take on this work and, since they do not have the financial support of a community of religious sisters or brothers, these lay people need to be paid, in order to eat. How is this going to be done? I see this as one of the most serious issues facing the authority church today.

To say that lay people need to be paid is not for a moment to take from the extraordinary generosity manifested by those same people; for the most part I believe that anyone who opts to work full-time in the church is hardly aiming to become a millionaire. The generosity with which people work in the church is evident in very many spheres – and by much more than lay people. One of the most heartening things for me in recent years has been seeing the considered and deliberate decisions by certain religious orders to work for and with and beside the poor. These, it seems to me, are the people who at this time in history are carrying on the work of Christ. (I am always astounded when I hear criticism of someone like Mother Teresa of Calcutta because 'she is not doing enough' or 'not doing things the right way'; at least she is trying).

When religious orders are joined in their work by lay people, it seems to me to be the most significant moving back in our own time to the origins of Christ's church. And it would seem today that in this lay movement lies our best hope of keeping Christ's word alive. It is certainly not new in our own country, given the extraordinary work done by people like Frank Duff, the founder of the Legion of Mary, much earlier in this century. But today there does seem to be a new surging forth of committed lay people who recognise the needs of today and who are prepared to give much, to learn much, and to enter into the arena of working for Christ at a very deep level. And it really is time that this great movement was appreciated by the powers that be. Surely the church authorities must rejoice that such a movement exists, especially given the huge falling-off in what was generally known as 'religious vocations'. Even the most traditional seem to accept – as they must, given the evidence before their eyes – that vocations as we knew them are fast disappearing; not completely, because there will no doubt always be those who will seek a life of withdrawal and prayer, but the numbers of religious in teaching and other active roles will probably never revert to what it was just a few decades ago.

Without doubt the changes have been monumental, and as an example I could cite the change within my own and the next generation. I believe it is true to say that when I left school, many of the families I knew had one child, and perhaps more than one, who chose to enter religious life.

In my own children's generation, I cannot think of even five families where there has been such a vocation. And all the statistics prove that this is so. Some lament this, while others see it as inevitable. And all sorts of reasons are proffered for this state of affairs; no doubt the scandals within our own church in more recent years make up part of the reason.

Whether you lament this falling off, see it as inevitable, or welcome it, the fact is that it is real, regardless of how we may feel about it, and those of us who are interested in – who love – the church need to accept the challenge and to try to meet it as best we may. And this takes vision.

Vision is not confined to the wearers of Roman collars. Vision comes to different people in different ways. Surely it is becoming obvious to the authorities in the Christian church today that they must set about involving the laity – Pobal Dé, the People of God – in the search for a way forward, entering into dialogue with them, learning from them and listening to their vision of what the church of the future might be.

Is it not time that the matter of ordination to the diaconate were high on the agenda? I have heard much discussion recently on the wonderful work being done at present by married deacons in the Church of England. Could not my own church learn anything from this? Is there so much to fear? Surely there is room for this ministry to be fully exercised once more, where people could be specially ordained to the diaconate in order that they might carry out certain priestly functions? What threat is to be found in such an idea?

(No doubt there are those who would argue that full diaconate – especially for women – would be a very dangerous thing indeed – the thin end of the wedge, so to speak. But so what? Wedges, like everything else, were invented in the first place because they served a useful purpose).

In the March 1995 edition of *The Furrow,* there were two articles pertaining to lay ministry, one giving the results of a survey recently carried out on that same subject and the other giving a commentary on those results. Having read both articles, I was left with a feeling of great sadness. Both confirmed that 'it is difficult to see a future for full-time non-ordained ministry in Ireland'. One of the authors also commented, '...the reluctance of authorities to establish lay people in voluntary non-ordained ministries... would seem to suggest that the key factor is control, not finance'. (I might question that one.) Another comment was, 'A related matter is whether or not the church can afford to pay lay people an adequate wage.' I ask: can it afford not to? How long, I wonder, will we as church blandly write, and blandly read, the results of surveys which state that '37% (of lay ministers) receive no payment for their work' or 'only 20% (of lay people) receive a proper salary' when working for the church, and leave such statements there as if they were nothing to worry about? Recently I heard a lawyer speaking on television about the judiciary, and he made the remark that our judiciary in Ireland was a good one and 'it costs what it costs'. He would brook no haggling with regard to the necessity for paying people what was necessary in order to ensure that the right people would be in appropriate positions. Surely he has a point. How can a church (and one, incidentally, which shows very little signs of being poor) say that it cannot afford to pay lay people to minister? It makes no sense. And it is, I believe, one of the most difficult subjects that my own church has to address. If we as church continue not to pay lay people who minister, then it can hardly surprise us that more than 21,000 people in Ireland recently signed their names to a petition for the lifting of the ban on the ordination of women; it may well follow that if ordination is what it takes to be allowed to minister *and to eat,* then there may well be some people who may find themselves going forward for ordination when in fact they might be much better suited to lay ministry.

The Sacrament of the Sick – a case in point

Because I trained as a hospital chaplain, I have a very keen interest in the Sacrament of the Sick. And, try as I might, I cannot see why this sacrament cannot be administered by a lay person. Surely if a lay person may baptise, it should also be possible for her/him to sacramentally anoint someone who is seriously ill. And surely also, since by and large it is women who care on a daily basis for the sick and dying, it would be entirely appropriate that they could also anoint those same people? In heaven's name, why not?

During my hospital chaplaincy training, there were times when it seemed to me that it would have been completely appropriate for me to have anointed someone to whom I was ministering, sometimes over an extended period. But in each case I had to seek out an ordained priest – often-times a stranger to the patient – to come and administer this sacrament. It seemed to me to be totally at odds with what ministry should be about. I wonder why we, as church, proclaim rules that don't stand up in practice? To do so undermines all the rules.

On one occasion, in the hospital to which I was attached, I was bringing Communion to a large ward. In order to reach this ward I had to pass some single rooms to which I did not have access, as the people in them were generally too ill to receive. On this particular day, however, as I was making my way past the rooms, a middle-aged woman ,who had been sitting on a chair outside one of the rooms, suddenly rushed over to me and said 'My daughter is dying'. (Familiar words.) 'Could you', she asked me, 'bring her Communion? She wishes for it.' I turned to the young nurse who was accompanying me on the round, as is the practice, and I asked her if she would enquire from the staff in the room of the dying girl if it might be possible for me to do so. She entered the room quickly and quickly returned, nodding her head vigorously, and so the patient's mother and I went in.

I saw – I can still see – the face of a young girl, who might have been eighteen years of age, or even twenty-eight, and there were three nurses standing around her bed. She was in distress, and the nurses were doing everything in their power to alleviate her pain. I remember being very frightened – I had probably never before been so near anyone who was dying. The senior nurse said to me, 'Please break off a tiny piece of the host, that is all she will manage.' This I did, and looked at the nurse enquiringly. She shook her head. 'Too big', she said. Three times I broke off a smaller piece, each time consuming the other small piece myself. Eventually the nurse allowed me to place a piece of the host no bigger than the head of a pin on the girl's tongue. With her eyes and her hands she thanked me, as she could not speak. I offered Communion to each of the nurses, and each received, as did the girl's mother. We stayed in the room in silence for some moments and then I left, and I know that I was very shaken. The girl's mother left with me, and asked me to return when I had finished the round, which I did.

Going back to the chapel I was still accompanied by the young nurse carrying a small light, as was the custom. She, instead of placing the light at the end of the chapel and leaving me to continue up to the altar to put away the ciborium, turned to me and said, 'I just want to say that I don't go in for religion and stuff like that, and I've often done this Communion round before, but I never remember a round like today's, and that young girl receiving Communion.' And I could see that she had been very affected by the incident, just as I had myself.

And afterwards I wondered just what was different about that Communion round for that young nurse from all the other rounds which she must have made in the course of her training. Was it possible – and I think it was – that as a mother I had a better chance of understanding what the mother of that dying girl was going through – understanding as perhaps only another mother could? Did the fact that I myself have five healthy children, all full of life, two of them daughters either of whom might have been the same age as the dying girl, make it possible for me to relate to the horror and pain that the woman was experiencing just then? I am not suggesting that a man might not have carried out these functions fully and meaningfully, but perhaps there are times when it is right and fitting that a minister be able to relate completely to another, as I believed happened on that occasion. Again, I am reminded of Mary and Elizabeth, and the fact that Mary wanted to share her extraordinary news with another woman. Might there not be times when it would be appropriate for a woman to administer the last rites? I am sure that it is so.

The following day I learned that the lovely young girl had died some hours after having received Communion from me. By coincidence, therefore, I had given her 'Food for the Journey'. Would it not have been reasonable for me to have been free to administer the Last Rites to her also, had I been asked? I believe it would, and I think this is well illustrated in the following story, which is also a true one.

There were two women, both in their early fifties, who had been great friends all their lives. One of them was dying, over a protracted period. When her illness struck for what turned out to be the last time, she was attending a Liturgy College, because liturgy was her great love, and it seemed a good place for her to spend the remainder of her rapidly ebbing life. Up to the day that she was admitted to hospital for the last time, during Easter Week, she was completely immersed in preparation for the Easter ceremonies. It broke her heart when she found that she would be unable to take part in them.

On Easter Sunday, when the ceremonies were over, her class mates arrived into the hospital ward and presented her with the blessed oils from their ceremonies, and that evening she requested that her friend should anoint her with the blessed oil, and that she should do likewise for her friend. And for the remaining days of her life they solemnly anointed each other every evening before parting.

But she was also, as she herself put it, 'of a legalistic turn of mind', and, for that reason, some weeks before her death she asked a priest whom she knew well to anoint her sacramentally. There was great discussion, and not a little sadness amongst the three of them, that it was not possible for her woman friend to administer the sacrament to her, which would have been the logical follow-up to the months of companionship which had gone before. The priest, fully aware of this, involved everyone as much as he could.

It so happened that the day of the 'official' anointing was very hot, and a small fly had come in the window of the ward. Fearing infection and further discomfort for the patient, her woman friend became obsessed with making sure that the fly was kept at a distance, when necessary waving her arms to prevent it from alighting on the patient. When the prayers were over, the priest, before putting away his missal, pointed to the page from which he had been reading and said in a solemn voice, 'And it says here, in red print, that the lay woman may swat flies!' Light relief, and both welcome and necessary at that point, but it did, I think, point up the absurdity of some of our man-made rules. If these two women had been ministering to each other for the greater part of their lives, and particularly during the most recent difficult times, surely it was a nonsense that their mutual ministering could not have incorporated the sacramental moment also, that moment which is inextricably part of the whole journey? It seems obvious to me that here is one sacrament which surely need not be the preserve of the ordained only – as, for example, baptism is not.

To my mind, this example shows at a practical level just how clumsy and unworkable some of the present rules are, and that very clumsiness would seem to me to indicate that they need to be looked at again, in the light of lived experience. This brings us into very theological territory concerning the origins of the sacrament, of priesthood itself, and the variety of interpretations of some of the gospel material on which they are based. I do not feel that this is the place to go into them in depth, but a couple of years ago I came across an excellent book on the subject of the origin of the Sacrament of the Sick – and indeed it touches also on the origins of the other sacraments and of the ordained priesthood too. The author, theologian John J. Ziegler, in *Let Them Anoint the Sick*, deals in great detail with the various Councils and Synods which took place since the beginnings of the church, and, despite all the rules made at various times during those Synods, comes out strongly in support of allowing lay ministers to anoint the sick and dying. (*Let Them Anoint the Sick*, John J. Ziegler, 1987, Liturgical Press, Minnesota). The logic of his arguments attracts me, and when I add his arguments to my own lived experience and to the experience of others to whom I have talked on the subject, I can only believe that there are indeed no good grounds for insisting that only an ordained person may anoint someone who is dying.

By tackling such questions then, perhaps we can begin, as Brendan Lovett suggests, to 'peel back the layers'. There will inevitably be pain, but that is not sufficient reason for us not to try.

Administering the Sacrament of the Sick to someone who is very ill and/or dying is only one aspect of this very particular, one-to-one ministry, this ministry which I believe best emulates the ministry of Jesus, because throughout his life Jesus ministered to the marginalised, and anyone who is ministering to a person who is dying is doing just that. A person who knows that she/he is terminally ill is marginalised in a very real sense, and there is, I believe, a terrible loneliness in that knowledge – and not only for the one who is dying.

For everyone involved, one of the most painful aspects of this knowledge is that the loneliness cannot be completely taken away, no matter what love there may be between the carer(s) and the stricken. To want to help, and to experience one's limitations in this regard is to understand and experience the poverty of the human. It brings with it real pain, the type of pain that must have been with Jesus when he hung on the cross, and with his mother as she stood beneath him. Neither could take away the other's pain, and this must have compounded their own.

There is a most moving section in C. S. Lewis's book, *A Grief Observed*, in which he gives an account of the dying and death of his young wife, from cancer, and this within a very short time of their marriage. He recounts how she once said to him, 'Even if we both died at exactly the same moment, as we lie side by side, it would be just as much of a separation...' It is true, of course. If two people die simultaneously, their journey into the unknown is still made separately. And that, I suppose, is what we are all afraid of when we admit to being afraid of dying, this 'aloneness'. I am reminded yet again of the 'separateness' of giving birth, and I believe that it is something akin.

But despite this separateness I also believe that it is possible to travel quite a long way down the road with someone who is dying; not all the way, obviously, but quite a distance. And this I see as the essence of ministry. This ministry, at a crucial time in someone's life, is not easy, but for all that it is an extraordinarily privileged place in which to find oneself, leading to a deepening and a stretching of all that has gone before in matters of faith.

I believe also that to undertake this kind of ministry means that one is taking on a poverty for oneself which is second to none, because it means two things: being very available, and, harder still, recognising one's limitations. Someone ministering to the dying also needs time out, that is essential. We have only to read the gospels to learn that Jesus himself, this man who was so available to so many during his public life, often 'withdrew', no doubt to re-charge his batteries, ground himself, take stock and pray. Everyone caring for another needs this – the more so, I believe, if they are walking the road with a terminally ill person. At a practical level it is probably essential that there be put in place a means for this time out to happen – and for someone else to take on this 'stand-by' role is surely a ministry in itself.

It may be that spouses or partners who have been together for a considerable time are in the most advantageous position to journey with another at this critical time, but this doesn't always follow. On the other hand, I believe it is also true that sometimes two people who may not have had the smoothest of relationships over the years may well find the resources within themselves to carry out this one-to-one ministry when 'the chips are down' for one of them.

But what of those who live alone, or who may find themselves to be alone even though a member of a large religious congregation? There is nothing new in saying here that it is not just the shortage of religious vocations which is resulting in many members of religious orders opting to live in groups of threes and fours, in 'family size' houses. I believe that this is coming about also because the need for intimacy has been seen to be one of great importance in the living out of our lives most fully, and that this possibility was sometimes, maybe often, lacking in larger religious establishments.

This is not to say that there will not always be those who choose to live lives of solitude. I remember being very moved some years ago when I heard a Benedictine monk say on radio that to him the vow of poverty 'means more than lack of worldly riches: it means having no-one with whom to share my life'. 'It is not good for (man) to be alone' was not said for nothing.

So, where does that leave those who may not have someone very close to them on whom to lean during the crisis of a perhaps long-drawn-out terminal illness?

It has been my experience that it is not always the most obvious person who turns out to be the principal carer. Sometimes it may be that even when it appears to the world in general that someone is surrounded by those who love her or him, there may in fact be no one, over and above the rest, who can fill this role. And it is precisely for this reason that I think we are asked, as part of our Christian living, to be at the ready; we simply don't know when we may be asked to undertake such a journey with another.

There is a rather simple story told of how two strangers walked towards Jerusalem hoping to find Jesus, because they had heard so much about him. As they neared the walls of the city they encountered a local coming walking towards them, and they asked her, 'Where might we find Jesus, and how will we recognise him?' And she, pointing to a group of dirty, ragged people near the gate, all wounded, some on crutches, some on stretchers, all with bandaged limbs, said to them 'Go over to that group of cripples, he is among them; and you will recognise him because, although both his hands are bleeding, only one of them is bandaged; he bandages them one at a time so that one hand is always free to help to bandage the wounds of the person next to him.'

A simple story, maybe, but I find that it makes the point for me: we simply don't know, no matter what worries we ourselves may have, just when we will be called on to help someone in far greater difficulties than we are in. And that same story also brings to my mind the title of Henri Neuwen's book, *The Wounded Healer*. He, too, tells us that this is the best we can hope to be; we are all wounded in one way or another, but there may be someone right beside us, known to us or a stranger, who may need us, for however brief or long a time, to walk with them in so far as we humanly can. We have to be at the ready. It may be costly, but because of what it is, the cost mustn't count. This is, I think, to learn the real meaning of the message of Jesus, and also to learn what is meant by unconditional love.

Nor is ministering ever, I believe, only one way. In all ministering there is a ceaseless flowing, back and forth, from one to the other. For all that a carer might undertake for someone who is very ill and /or dying, you may be sure that the ministering is being reciprocated. I am again reminded of my – limited – experience in hospital wards. Nothing is surer but that those to whom I tried to minister ministered to me in return, and at the very least one hundredfold.

And whenever I think of the reciprocity of ministry I find myself reminded yet again of the woman at the well, and her encounter with Jesus. Here was the most marvellous opening gambit on his part, showing how well he under-stood the need to recognise the mutuality of ministry. He actually puts himself at the receiving end, giving her the opportunity to minister to him, in order to pave the way so that he might minister to her at an even deeper level; no wonder the well is the symbol in this story. I think that the psychology behind his simple request for a drink of water was masterful; it opened up the endless possibilities which followed; she couldn't refuse him, and the results reached into infinity.

Even in the most unlikely situations, ministry brings reci-procity in its wake. A parent ministering to an infant's every need will also experience the two-way movement of grace, as wonder and love flow from the infant in return. Even in this improbable place the adult also receives.

There is another side to all of this; it is one thing to be ready to minister to a loved one; it is quite another to be separated from that loved one when he or she may be in crisis and needing help. Not to be available, whether for geographical or other reasons, can be extraordinarily painful. But I think it often happens that if we ourselves cannot be there, for whatever reason, then someone else will take our place. Indeed, this is not without its pain also, the knowledge that someone else is where we most want to be. It can even happen that someone else will be pre-ferred – 'the most unkindest cut of all' – but unconditional love will let that pass.

I remember something the late Peter Lemass wrote when he had somewhat recovered from one stage of the cruel ill-ness which took him to his too-early death a decade ago. He had gone through great suffering in hospital, his skin having broken down because of an allergy, and, writing about this later in *The Furrow,* he said of his time in the

Intensive Care Unit, 'Each time a nurse went off duty I suffered withdrawal symptoms.' He was so completely dependent for all his needs on each one of the staff that as each shift of personnel took place he suffered intensely. That was dependency. That was pain. Yet I know that if you were to meet any one of those nurses today, a decade later, she would probably tell you of the depth of Peter's ministry to her, even during those weeks. That was reciprocity in ministry.

This extraordinary generosity of spirit, which manifests itself in such powerful ways through humanity is one of the Creator's greatest gifts to us. It is boundless; it stretches from one side of the globe to the other. And it is our hope, that towards which we dare to reach, in whatever stumbling fashion we may. And surely it is from the knowledge that such love exists that we must take heart. If we profess to believe in the communion of saints – saints with a small 's' – and if we ourselves cannot be present with someone we love when they are going through a difficult time, then we must hope and pray that someone else is there in our stead. And if we find this painful, then so be it. To quote Brendan Lovett again: 'To say "Yes" to life, to receive it as gift, is to accept everything as an interconnected unity.' Years ago I read: 'It is one of the tragedies of life that very often those whom we love most are not with us when we most need them – and one of the glories that they sometimes are.' There is great wisdom in those words.

Such ministering as I have described above is obviously not confined to the ordained. In many cases it may well be that a lay person will be the appropriate person to fill the role. It would be wonderful if the church authorities would begin to recognise this fact and enable lay people to take their place alongside the ordained in certain situations. I am convinced that if this could be achieved it would enrich our needy church beyond recognition just now.

CHAPTER 6

Collaborative ministry: the way forward

Except in some exceptional cases the 'other' usually appears to be the worst danger that our personality meets in the whole course of its development. The other is a nuisance. The other must be got out of the way. The persons in the street get in my way because I collide with them as possible rivals. I shall like them as soon as I see them as partners in the struggle.

— Teilhard de Chardin, *Human Energy*.

Not for nothing we were told, at the conference to which I referred at the beginning of this book, that 'forgiveness is the air we breathe'.

For so it is. So is everything. Today, just before taking up my pen, I was hanging clothes out on the line in the garden and quite suddenly I became aware of the heat in the air and the amazing stillness in which everything was wrapped. Not a leaf stirred, and I realised that I couldn't even hear the distant sound of traffic; the silence was broken only by the low hum of an industrious bee as it went from blossom to blossom doing all it had to do – and to perfection. For a moment I was bowled over by beauty: the greenness of the small patch of grass where daisies grew in abundance – no magazine-cover garden this! – the utter stillness of the leaves on the somewhat straggly branches of the apple tree; the vivid yellow of a rose beside me; the heavy scent of a summer's day. And all of this given to us regardless of our failings; love 'poured out', surrounding us on all sides, unceasingly and in profusion, in all that we can see and hear and feel and smell and touch; in music, in language, and – for me always most marked of all – in the love of friends.

I knew that I was caught into one of those blessed moments, gifts themselves, when a heightened awareness told me at first hand and absolutely that forgiveness enfolded me – and what is more, I felt able to accept this fact.

Of course I also knew that this understanding might not last – we are fickle, fearful, doubting creatures most of the time, I think – but at least for that instant I thought I understood something. Patrick Kavanagh expresses it most wonderfully:

> Yet sometimes when the sun comes through the gap
> These men know God the father in a tree:
> The Holy Spirit is the rising sap,
> and Christ will be the green leaves that will come
> At Easter from the sealed and guarded tomb.
> (*The Great Hunger*)

It follows, surely, that if we are forgiven, then we in turn must forgive. We must forgive those who trespass against us – or those whom we perceive so to do; and we must forgive ourselves.

How better to go about this then, than by entering into collaborative ministry, each with the other?

We simply cannot afford not to look for ways in which to do this, because unless we do then there will be, as some theologians have been heard to say, no future for the church.

It also seems perfectly logical, again as mentioned earlier, that in order to deal with something we must be able to name it. And it seems to me that one of the vital things which appears to be missing today within the church is collaboration between the ordained and the non-ordained. The quotation from Chardin with which I have prefaced this chapter is probably as true with regard to relationships within our church today as it is about most situations throughout the world where there is unease, antagonism or even outright war. The problem is fear of the other. And fear of the other always seems to be where there is a lack of knowing. In order, then, to be rid of such fear, we need knowledge of the other. And yet that very fear prevents us from seeking out that knowledge. Thus we end up in a sort of vicious circle, or catch-22 situation.

Despite this however – or maybe because of it – I think it might be useful to try to name some of the ways in which collaborative ministry might be undertaken by all of us, in order that we might move forward.

I am sure that to bring this about the greatest changes will have to be made by those in authority; many members of the laity are ready. And it is undoubtedly going to involve the powers that be facing up to the fact that they act unjustly towards women. One of the difficulties, I suspect, may well be that many of them are aware of this, but feel unable to grapple with the problem.

I think that a good way to get over this inhibition is to look at the question in the context of justice. It has to be plain to many in authority that to tell women that they are equal to men on the one hand, and on the other to say to them 'Do not dare to break the Bread, anoint the sick or forgive in his name' is not only unjust, but also in direct contradiction to the teachings of Jesus, who sought at every opportunity to release women from subordination. It has been particularly difficult for many, men as well as women, to understand the recent letter of the present pontiff and the subsequent statement from the Congregation for the Doctrine of the Faith pertaining to women and ordination, both of which state that all the faithful must hold the view that women can never be ordained, not now nor in the future, to the priesthood. There are very many who in good conscience find this impossible. How have the church authorities backed themselves into such a corner that they believe such a statement can be acceptable to thinking adults?

Has the making of such statements come about because of the fear the authority church has of women? And if so, what can be done to alleviate such fear?

I am very conscious of the fact that it is probably a lot easier for me to make suggestions about all of this than it might be for someone who is ordained, and 'caught into the system'. It is for this reason that I make them.

So I would begin, then, with a relatively 'easy' subject, but one which would give a lot of encouragement to people if changes were to be made, and that is the matter of liturgies. What is to prevent women being much more visibly involved in all liturgies, at a much deeper level than is at present the case? In the case of the eucharist, for example, why cannot a women read the gospel? It would seem to make a great deal of sense that, especially when the passages refer to women, a woman might be the reader – say, at the story of the annunciation, or the woman at the well, or Mary and Martha; or the haemorrhaging woman; or the woman who anointed Jesus. The opportunities are certainly there.

And, following on that, why should not a woman give the homily? Surely it makes sense that the gospel stories would be looked at from a woman's point of view – just as much as from a man's – and shared with others? I met a woman coming out of Mass not many months ago, where we had been subjected to a fifteen-minute homily by a no doubt very well-meaning priest on the pain involved in having children! She told me that it took all her strength not to stand up and say, 'Hang on a minute! I'll take this one!' And what would have been wrong with that? Nothing whatever, of course, but unhappily many of us as yet lack that sort of courage. (Perhaps not for long more!)

But to make these changes, and to enable women to find this kind of courage, does mean that celebrants would have to stand up and be counted, by inviting women to join in in this way. And so what? If a celebrant were to invite a woman in his parish to read the gospel and to give the homily from time to time, it seems highly unlikely that the sky would fall in. Someone has to start – and it cannot be a lay person.

Again, my mind goes back to hospital chaplaincy appointments. One way round the exclusion of women from paid hospital chaplaincy work would seem to me to be the following: let each ordained who is offered such a position accept only on condition that a lay person is appointed alongside him, and under the same conditions. This would sort that matter out. But again, it is the ordained who have the power to make the change. Again, it means standing up and being counted.

And what about the matter of changing to inclusive language? How about those who are ordained making a conscious effort to speak of God as feminine – if they are not doing so already? It is often argued that language doesn't matter, but this is untrue. It may well not matter to many, but there are others to whom it matters greatly and they must be taken into consideration. To say that language doesn't matter is, as I see it, the same as saying to someone who has no money that money doesn't matter; it doesn't – so long as it's there. But ask those without, and you will find that it matters very much indeed. So it is with inclusive language. I am convinced that if the female pronoun were to be used exclusively when speaking of God, many men would be highly offended.

(It might be worth trying this out at official liturgies. I am fairly sure that it will not pass off smoothly, for the most part).

These are only a couple of examples where collaborative ministry might begin, and there are undoubtedly more. However, while these would help, they are not by any means the most important steps that have to be taken. The most important step, I am convinced, is that each person in authority in the church begin to sit down, one to one, with a woman of his acquaintance, and say to her, 'Tell me your experience – of womanhood, of church, of the world, of God; tell me what it feels like, from your point of view.' This I see as the most vital step. And, when he has heard, let him then reflect deeply on how he might, in however small a way, involve that woman in ministry alongside himself. There's no point in leaving it to the man in the next parish. And don't worry about risk; nothing is surer than that it takes risk to make a difference. Chance it.

And, if you haven't started already, begin to read some feminist theologians. Read Joan Chittister, Sandra Schneiders, Rosemary Haughton, Sallie MacFague, Edwina Gateley, Anne Thurston. Read what they are saying, and then deliberately meditate on their words, linking their experiences with the stories of Jesus and the women he encountered. Start making the connections; begin to notice the way in which Jesus broke the man-made rules in order to make sure that everyone would be included. And start doing the same yourself.

Study Jesus' ancestors on the female side; contemplate the female line from which he was descended, born of Mary, a descendant of Ruth, of Leah, of Rebekah, of Sarah; and ask yourself why we hear so little of these matters. Ask yourself what it might be like today if, 2,000 years ago women had known how to read and write; how might the gospel stories have differed? Would we know the name, for instance, of the woman who poured the oil over him? Would we have got a different slant on things if that woman had been able to write down her memories? Or if her mother or a sister had? The chances are that if that had been so, we would at least have been told her name.

Begin to understand that the world, and the Christian churches along with the world, look on the male species as being definitively human, and, as Aquinas so succinctly put it, females as 'flawed males'. Try to imagine what it must be like to know that one is part of the species which is believed to be 'flawed'. And think about the fact that, far from following the world in this matter, it is up to the Christian churches, in the name of their founder, to give the lead in breaking through this sinful attitude to women – for that is what it is.

Begin, if you will, to reflect on the fact that Jesus came on earth as human, rather than thinking of his gender. And think about the fact that we are all, by baptism, called to be Christ to one another. And think of what a waste it is that so many are denied the chance to respond directly to this call, because of man-made rules which exclude them from full ministry.

I once heard a lecturer say, 'Jesus said "Think, think, think!"' I'm sure he was right.

And if the matter of involving women visibly in liturgies proves too daunting, then at least look for other ways in which you, as an ordained priest, can collaborate with lay people. Collaboration can exist – and often does – in quieter ways. Recently there was a very interesting suggestion in a letter to *The Furrow* from the mother of a family, and she asked that the church authorities might give thought to the possibility of a celebrant of the eucharist at a special family occasion giving general absolution to all present, so that all would feel free, if they so wished, to receive communion, regardless of their 'official' standing in the church in connection with, perhaps, 'legal' status *vis a vis* marriage laws, both secular and religious. It is so often the case now that the younger generation, for what appear to them to be good reasons, may not be as committed to church and other legalities concerning their partnerships, as their parents were. It can often, as the writer to *The Furrow* points out, be painful for many if, at a family gathering, some members of the family and perhaps the celebrant also feel constrained, thereby creating a dividing line between members of the same family at the very time when the liturgy could be a healing and unifying event. We certainly never heard that Jesus said to anyone, 'You can't eat with the rest of us', no matter what the circumstances were; in fact, great care has been taken to tell us that he sat down to eat with everyone, going out of his way to ensure that table fellowship was extended to the most unlikely, the most marginalised. Why do we do things differently, when he has set such example? Can we not make better efforts to emulate him in this very important matter?

I am sure that there are many ordained who do involve all family members in this way on special occasions, but perhaps many more could also see the wisdom of so doing. This in itself would be a wonderful way of collaboration, especially with parents who are often making heroic efforts, and sometimes in difficult circumstances, to make sure that no family member will feel excluded from the table at important family times. I know many parents who would find collaboration of this kind most helpful.

CHAPTER 7

Fringe Benefits?

Freedom does not thrive on set ways of doing things.
— Hugo Echegarary, *The Practice of Jesus.*

Naïvely perhaps, I assumed that this would constitute a chapter at least the same length as the other chapters. The first thing I discovered was that it would be a short one, and the second was that on writing down the words 'Fringe Benefits' I then needed to add a question mark.

It seems to me that the only obvious benefit about being on the fringe, when one would prefer to be involved, is that one is free to speak one's mind. If, as a woman, I cannot become wholeheartedly involved in ministry within my church, then I can at least express my disappointment and my acute sense of injustice which I perceive to be visited on me and other women who are excluded from full ministry on gender grounds. There has to be anger too, since injustice necessarily involves anger, although not exclusively. And anyway, anger is by no means always a negative thing. Sometimes it is energising.

If we are not permitted to become involved at the deepest level in ministry, then we are certainly free to say what this means to us.

There must have been a myriad reasons why Jesus spent the first thirty years of his earthly life in the obscurity of the home he shared for all of that time with his mother. And one of the most useful things he must have learned

from her during that time was that there is value in reflecting. Women are often good at reflecting, and sometimes I
can see that one reason for this is that many of the tasks
which women do in their everyday lives – tasks such as
ironing, peeling potatoes, dusting, sweeping – are repetitive tasks, which at least to some extent leave the mind free
to dwell on other things. (I know that certain schools of
psychology might say that to give one's whole attention to
the ironing, or the sweeping, or the dusting, might behove
one better; in my experience, however, in practice it is
often possible to get on with the task, and mull over something entirely different at the same time.) I find that I enjoy
the 'pace' of the painting by William Orpen in the National
Gallery in Dublin, entitled 'The Washouse', because I can
almost feel the repetitive motion of the wash-girl's arms as
she immerses the clothes in the tub of water and then lifts
them out again. There is another lovely painting by the
American painter, John Sargent, called 'The Bead Stringers',
and this I also find contemplative, for the same reasons.
Such rhythmic gestures invite contemplation.

As a rule, thinking things through often brings much questioning in its wake. That's its value. We go through the
process of thinking, and the questions invariably form,
sometimes one after the other after the other. And this is
the endless quest for the truth. Joan Chittister says, in *The
Fire in these Ashes*, 'We must go from answer to answer till
we find the whole truth. We must learn to question and we
must learn to search. Obedience is not about childish de-
pendence, however trusting; obedience is about life gone
wild with the personal awareness of personal responsibility'. And this sounds right to me.

We who question can take comfort, I believe, in remember-
ing that Jesus never ceased to ask questions in his dealings
with others, whether in his compassionate questioning of
the woman who was being stoned, 'Is there no-one left to

condemn you?', his somewhat sharp questioning of his mother on more than one occasion, 'Did you not know that I must be about my Father's business?', or, 'What is that to you and to me?' at the wedding feast of Cana; or, most telling of all in demonstrating his complete humanity, his questioning of Peter: 'Do you love me?' He asked questions because he wanted to get to the heart of things. So do we who ask questions today. It seems, therefore, that we are in good company.

Women are not involved in decision-making in the church; for the most part they are not valued; for the most part they may find it extremely difficult to feel any sense of belonging; they can usually find no place where they can express their views and feel that anyone is listening to them; for all those reasons and many more, it seems that they might as well take on the role of persistent questioners – as, indeed, many are now doing.

We must take advantage of this leeway, it seems to me, and find ways and means of being church – ways and means that mean something to us as women. For a start, we can create our own liturgies – as many women are already doing – liturgies to which we ourselves can relate with ease, and of which we can feel a part. Most importantly, we can look to our fellow Christian women of other denominations and learn from them. It has occurred to me on numerous occasions that the uniting of the Christian churches will probably be brought about through and by women in ministry, because many women do not have the time to agonise over esoteric points of obscure theology when they want to get on with their daily living in a way that seeks to emulate the founder of Christianity. They want to get on with things at a practical level, as the deepest expression of Christian love. They want to feed the hungry, clothe the poor, visit the sick. They want to understand scripture from their own point of view. Women know that washing, holding, comforting the bodies of the sick, the helpless and the dying, is in itself sacramental. They know that this is where ministry is; that to look after another – or be looked after – at such a level is precisely what Christians are called to do when they are called to be Christ to one another. For the most part, it is women who are the midwives, helping others to give birth, and who help others on the last lonely journey; surely these are reasons enough for bringing them into full involvement into the various ministries in the church? And not for a moment am I suggesting that these ministries are for women alone, far from it. Women need the collaboration of their fellow pilgrims who are men, just as much as the other way around. Thank heavens it is coming about, however slowly, that some men are beginning to understand how greatly the church is impoverishing itself by failing to make room for its female members in all its ministries at every level in its day-to-day running.

But since the change does not automatically happen, since in this as in many other matters movement within the church authoritites is sluggish, then it would seem that constant questioning is a necessary part of some people's role in the church today. It may not always be comfortable, either for the questioners or for those who are questioned, but it is still necessary. In his lovely book, *The Small Hours of Belief*, Enda McDonagh speaks of this discomfort. He says '…we will often find ourselves at odds with one another, out of tune with the world. We will find ourselves, as Jesus did, thought perhaps by our families to be "beside ourselves"… We may look foolish, we may not sound sensible, but we could be the clown-creators who are… often rejected'. (*The Small Hours of Belief*, Enda McDonagh, Columba Press, 1989).

And he then, and I happily emulate him, quotes the following marvellous poem by E. E. Cummings:

a bespangled clown
standing on eighth street
handed me a flower.

Nobody, it's safe
to say, observed him but

myself; and why? because

without any doubt he was
whatever (first and last)

mostpeople fear most:
a mystery for which i've
no word except alive

—that is, completely alert
and miraculously whole;

with not merely a mind and a heart

but unquestionably a soul—
by no means funerally hilarious

(or otherwise democratic)
but essentially poetic
or ethereally serious:

a fine not a coarse clown
(no mob, but a person)

and while never saying a word

who was anything but dumb;
since the silence of him

self sang like a bird.
Mostpeople have been heard
screaming for international

measures that render hell rational
– I thank heaven somebody's crazy

enough to give me a daisy.

Perhaps betimes there's not much separating nuisances from clowns, and perhaps also, in the interests of balance, the world and the church need both.

Addendum

In November, 1996, B.A.S.I.C. – Brother and Sisters in Christ – launched a discussion document on women's ordination which was gladly received by many; ordained, non-ordained, members of various religious Orders. One theologian described it as 'admirable and impressive. It does not throw down the gauntlet but advances a tough challenge. It speaks with a voice of conviction without the rhetoric of partisanship.' Although regrettably without the very fine illustrations incorporated within it, the entire document is given hereunder, by kind permission of B.A.S.I.C..

Ordination of Women in the Catholic Church
Women – Called to be Priests
7 Questions for reflection, discussion and discernment

The call to ministerial priesthood comes from God and is a call to loving service

Q. 1. Did Jesus ordain only men?

There is no reference in scripture to Jesus ordaining anyone, male or female. In 1976 the Pontifical Biblical Commission set up by Paul VI to examine the scriptural evidence for the possibility of admitting women to the priesthood reported that there are no scriptural obstacles to the ordination of women.

It is important to know that 'Apostle' in its New Testament usage meant one who was a commissioned messenger. St

Paul was not one of the twelve, yet he clearly was an apostle, as was Barnabas. Romans 16 refers to a woman apostle, Junias. The twelve selected by Jesus are a prophetic sign of the new Israel, and are a clear reference to the twelve tribes from the twelve sons of Jacob in the Old Testament. There is no evidence that these twelve were the only ones present at the Last Supper. It is not unlikely that several of the women who had followed Jesus from Galilee were also present at the Last Supper, when Jesus asked his friends to celebrate his memory in the breaking of the bread.

Q. 2. Were women involved in the ministry of Jesus?

Yes, Jesus called both men and women to follow him.

One of the deepest theological dialogues in the New Testament occurs in John 4:1-42 where Jesus has a conversation with the Samaritan woman at the well and chooses to reveal himself to her as the Messiah. Luke mentions Mary, Joanna, Suzanna 'and some others who provided for them out of their own funds'. Martha professed Jesus as the Christ and her sister Mary sat at his feet to be instructed. It was a woman who anointed Jesus before his passion. Women were the ones who remained at the foot of the cross. Mary Magdalene was sent by the risen Christ to announce the news of his resurrection to the other disciples, 'I have seen the Lord, and this is what he said to me' (Jn 20:18). The church honours her as 'the apostle to the apostles'. And at Pentecost the Holy Spirit filled *both* the women *and* the men disciples (Acts 2).

Q. 3. Did women exercise leadership in the early New Testament communities?

Yes, the New Testament reveals that women had leadership roles in the early church.

Phoebe is a deacon and patron of the church at Cenchreae

(Rom 16:1-2) Chloe is the church leader at Corinth (1 Cor 1:11) Paul's co-workers are Mary, Tryphaena and Tryphosa (Rom 16:12) and Priscilla is a teacher, missionary and church leader (Acts 18:26, 1 Cor 16:19, Rom 16:3). These women exercised ministry, they spread the good news, brought Christ to a wider community in exactly the same way as the men.

Q. 4. How did the practice of excluding women from leadership in the church develop?

After an initial period of equality the church adopted the patriarchal structures of the world.

As the earliest Christian assemblies in house churches expanded, the contemporary models of male public leadership gradually took over.

The presiding elders (*presbyteroi*) or leaders came to be understood as being the exclusive representations of Christ, while before all the baptised were. Women were considered unable to be a sacramental sign of Christ and unfit for ordination. Yet in scripture we read that both men and women are created in the divine image (Gen 1:27), that there is no difference between men and women who are both baptised into Christ (Rom 8:29; 1 Cor 15:49; Col 3:10; 1 Jn 3:2) and that the Holy Spirit indwells all the disciples of Christ. Christian tradition, as well as society at large up to recent times, simply assumed the natural inferiority of women and therefore their incapacity for leadership. However, with Vatican II the church acknowledged the equality of men and women. In its 1973 decree *Mysterium Fidei*, (sic), the Congregation for the Doctrine of the Faith explicitly recognised the historical conditioning and therefore inherent limitations in the formation of church dogma, at any given period in history. May one not assume that past customs and usages which are today experienced as an obstruction to the gospel message, are subject to the same criteria?

Q. 5. Are there women who feel called to serve as priests?

Yes, there are many women in Ireland and throughout the world who believe that this is their vocation.

They are from all walks of life, and all ages. Some are married and some are single, some are religious. They are ordinary Christian women who have discovered in themselves a God-given desire to serve the Christian community in this way. In many cases this desire came as a disturbing surprise and they have struggled with it before welcoming it as 'good news' in their lives and the life of the church. Each has travelled a unique faith journey and brings unique gifts and experiences but all have in common a love for God and the church. This desire to be ordained is often dismissed as an individualistic quest for power rather than as a faithful response to God's initiative. St Thérèse of Lisieux can hardly be accused of such motives. Yet she both felt deeply the desire to be a priest and the pain of being denied ordination. A hundred years after her death Catholic women who live with the same desire and the same pain pray, work and hope that it may at last become possible.

Q. 6. Does the church need women priests?

Yes, the church needs women as priests, as it needs them in all areas of life, and it will be enriched by their presence and their gifts. Women image God and minister God's love in a way that a male-only priesthood cannot bear witness to.

While women are not to be ordained as an expedient to remedy the shortfall in male celibate vocations to the priesthood, the shortage of priests throughout the world is helping us to discover what God is doing in and through women. It is estimated that there are 400 million Catholics who are deprived of a regular celebration of the eucharist.

When they fail to recognise and affirm the many priestly vocations of women in their midst, church leaders are creating a eucharistic famine where God has provided in abundance.

Q. 7. The Pope has declared that 'the church does not have the authority to confer priestly ordination on women' and The Congregation for the Doctrine of the Faith claims that this is an infallible statement. What is the point then of further discussion?

The church's teaching and practice guided by the Holy Spirit have always remained open to further development in line with the criteria laid down in the decree *Mysterium Fidei* (see Q. 4 above).

And in this case theologians have pointed out that the Pope's statement does not meet the church's own strict criteria for infallibility.

No consultation has taken place with all the bishops of the church. An increasing number of the lay faithful believe that women should be ordained. The Holy Spirit is prompting people to continue to discuss and to debate the issue. Are we to refuse to interpret and live the gospel according to the 'signs of the times'? In conscience we cannot do so. What is urgently needed is for all church members to engage in prayerful dialogue, confident that the Spirit will lead us to the Truth.

* * *

What can I do to help women be ordained priests in the Roman Catholic Church?

7 Suggestions:

(1) Pray for church leaders and for ourselves that we may be fully attuned to the work of the Holy Spirit in the church and in the world.

(2) Pray for the women who are called to be priests. If you know any personally, let them know of your support for their vocation.

(3) Write to your priests and bishop expressing your concerns and your hopes.

(4) Read further on the issue (a full bibliography and more information is available from B.A.S.I.C.) and speak about it to family, friends, colleagues.

(5) Sign the B.A.S.I.C. petition. Over 20,000 people have already signed it.

(6) Become a member of B.A.S.I.C. and/or support our work with a donation – no matter how small.

(7) Call for the introduction of women deacons.

All ministry is by God's grace

'The following stress in the documents of Vatican II is consistently maintained. The call to ministry is ultimately not from a church official but from the Lord himself. The church officials must, of course, discern in faith whether the Lord is actually calling an individual or not, but the call and the commission is in the last analysis from the Lord. In today's world, it would seem, the Lord might indeed be calling a woman to priestly ordination. In other words, if the call is not directly from the bishop or some other church official, but from the Lord himself, and even the commissioning is from the Sacrament, not from delegation, and therefore, again, from the Lord himself, then great care must be exercised by all church officials in their discernment of Christ's call and commissioning. This is not to downplay the role of the church in the selection and ordination of ministers but it is rather a caution, based on the very theology of Vatican II, not to absolutise historical data.' — Kenan B. Osborne, OFM, *Priesthood – A History of the Ordained Ministry in the Roman Catholic Church*, (Paulist Press, New York/Mahwah, 1988), p. 354.

Copies of this document are available free of charge from B.A.S.I.C., 'St François', Avoca Avenue, Blackrock, Co Dublin. Tel: (01) 2885520.